The School Effectiveness Series

Foreword

A teacher's task is much more ambitious than it used to be and demands a focus on the subtleties of teaching and learning and on the emerging knowledge of school improvement.

This is what this series is about.

Teaching can be a very lonely activity. The time-honoured practice of a single teacher working alone in the classroom is still the norm; yet to operate alone is, in the end, to become isolated and impoverished. This series addresses two issues – the need to focus on practical and useful ideas connected with teaching and learning and the wish thereby to provide some sort of an antidote to the loneliness of the long-distance teacher who is daily berated by an anxious society.

Teachers flourish best when, in key stage teams or departments (or more rarely whole schools), their talk is predominantly about teaching and learning and where, unconnected with appraisal, they are privileged to observe each other teach; to plan and review their work together; and to practise the habit of learning from each other new teaching techniques. But how does this state of affairs arise? Is it to do with the way staffrooms are physically organised so that the walls bear testimony to interesting articles and in the corner there is a dedicated computer tuned to 'conferences' about SEN, school improvement, the teaching of English etc., and whether, in consequence, the teacher leaning over the shoulder of the enthusiastic IT colleague sees the promise of interesting practice elsewhere? Has the primary school cracked it when it organises successive staff meetings in different classrooms and invites the 'host' teacher to start the meeting with a 15 minute exposition of their classroom organisation and management? Or is it the same staff sharing, on a rota basis, a slot on successive staff meeting agenda when each in turn reviews a new book they have used with their class? And what of the whole school which now uses 'active' and 'passive' concerts of carefully chosen music as part of their accelerated learning techniques?

It is of course well understood that even excellent teachers feel threatened when first they are observed. Hence the epidemic of trauma associated with OFSTED. The constant observation of the teacher in training seems like that of the learner driver. Once you have passed your test and can drive unaccompanied, you do. You often make lots of mistakes and sometimes get into bad habits. Woe betide, however, the back seat driver who tells you so. In the same way, the new teacher quickly loses the habit of observing others and being observed. So how do we get a confident, mutual observation debate going? One school I know found a simple and therefore brilliant solution. The Head of the History Department asked that a young colleague plan lessons for her – the Head of Department – to teach. This lesson she then taught, and was observed by the young colleague. There was subsequent discussion, in which the young teacher asked,

> *"Why did you divert the question and answer session I had planned?"*

and was answered by,

> *"Because I could see that I needed to arrest the attention of the group by the window with some 'hands-on' role-play, etc."*

Adventures in Learning

This lasted an hour and led to a once-a-term repeat discussion which, in the end, was adopted by the whole school. The whole school subsequently changed the pattern of its meetings to consolidate extended debate about teaching and learning. The two teachers claimed that, because one planned and the other taught, both were implicated but neither alone was responsible or felt 'got at'.

So there are practices which are both practical and more likely to make teaching a rewarding and successful activity. They can, as it were, increase the likelihood of a teacher surprising the pupils into understanding or doing something they did not think they could do rather than simply entertaining them or worse still occupying them. There are ways of helping teachers judge the best method of getting pupil expectation just ahead of self-esteem.

This series focuses on straightforward interventions which individual schools and teachers use to make life more rewarding for themselves and those they teach. Teachers deserve nothing less, for they are the architects of tomorrow's society, and society's ambition for what they achieve increases as each year passes.

Professor Tim Brighouse

This book is to be returned on or before
the last date stamped below.

EDUCATION
COLLECTION

LIBREX

Library Services
Victoria Buildings
Queen Street
Falkirk
FK2 7AF

370
.152
3
TIL

Falkirk Council

FALKIRK COUNCIL
LIBRARY SUPPORT
FOR SCHOOLS

Mike Tilling

Published by Network Educational Press Ltd.
PO Box 635
Stafford
ST16 1BF

© Mike Tilling 2001

ISBN 1 85539 073 6

Mike Tilling asserts his moral right to be identified as
the author of this work.

All rights reserved. No part of this publication may be reproduced, stored
in a retrieval system or reproduced or transmitted in any form or by any
means, electronic, mechanical, photocopying, recording or otherwise,
without the prior written permission of the publishers. This book may not
be lent, resold, hired out or otherwise disposed of by way of trade in any
form of binding or cover other than that in which it is published without
the prior consent of the publishers.

Every effort has been made to contact copyright holders of materials
reproduced in this book. The publishers apologise for any omissions and
will be pleased to rectify them at the earliest opportunity.

Series Editor: Prof Tim Brighouse
Editor: Gina Walker
Design & layout: Neil Hawkins, Network Educational Press Ltd.
Illustrations: Barking Dog Art and Neil Hawkins

Printed in Great Britain by
MPG Books Ltd., Bodmin, Cornwall

Contents

For Jill, Frances and Jane

Overview

In Section One we learn that:

- Current models of learning tend to be limited to specific areas of the learning experience.

- A model based on narrative structures offers an overview of the learning process.

Most of us have theories about how learning happens. These are rarely explicit, and are usually shaped by personal experience, some knowledge of research in the subject and, if we are teachers, observation of what seems to work in lessons. In other words, we may have skills, subject knowledge and insight into the minds of individuals, but these are rarely integrated into a coherent system that can guide practice. Rather, they tend to be used to solve the very pressing and localised problems presented to teachers on a day-to-day basis.

Adventures in Learning offers a framework in which the intuitions of individual teachers can be synthesised into a broader understanding of how learning happens.

Learning is a complex process and no single model can explain what is meant when we say someone has 'learned' something. *Adventures in Learning* suggests a holistic model, which is not partial (in the sense that it does not rely on a single aspect of the learning process for its explanatory power), but strives to integrate a number of learning theories. It may be helpful to begin by thinking of learning as having four dimensions. Three of them may be characterised as:

- **learner attitude**, including motivation, emotion and temperament

- **learning strategy**, referring to the preferences that learners have for how they learn

- **learning channels**, which describe the learners' predilection for listening, speaking, reading, writing, watching or doing.

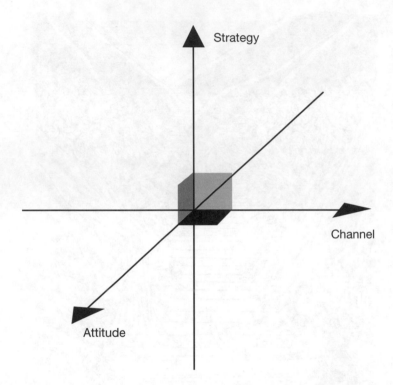

The fourth dimension may be represented by the notion of the **Learner's Journey**, which offers a metaphorical explanation and discusses how learning happens over time.

Clearly, there are other factors that may affect learning. For example, there are issues of *intelligence*, and *access* to resources. Many teachers would argue that *home background* is important, and it would be difficult to deny that *assessment methods* feed back into the process of learning. However, we are concerned here with deriving a model that relates to the processes of learning itself and relegates other factors, for the moment, to the background.

Stop and think: What is learning?
What do we mean when we say that someone has 'learned' something? When you have formed some ideas, try to arrange them into a hierarchy of importance.

Comment
Clearly, responses to this question will vary widely, but you may have written something like this.

When we say someone has learned something we mean that they have:
1   extended their knowledge
2   gathered some information into their short- and long-term memory
3   acquired skills that can be stored and used
4   found out how an idea or new understanding can change their life
5   understood reality.

There is a significant divide between items 1–3 and items 4–5 in this list. Points 1, 2 and 3 are all essential for learning, but they are qualitatively different from the last two. 1, 2 and 3 are concerned with reproducing information while 4 and 5 emphasise meaning and understanding. However, many learners do not progress beyond 'reproducing', to the higher level of 'meaning'. The success or failure of learners to make this leap of the imagination may be the result of their learning attitude.

Learner attitudes

Learners begin the Secondary phase of education carrying a certain amount of 'baggage'. Previous experiences will have shaped their attitude to learning. A simple way of representing this is a continuum running from 'deep' to 'surface' approaches. These orientations colour the processes of learning because they represent a personal construct of the learner's world.

Deep learning   Surface learning

In summary form, the two approaches may be characterised as follows.

Surface learners tend to:

- over-emphasise the importance of rote learning

- be particularly conscious of examination demands and assessment methods

- prefer to accumulate facts (the 'Mastermind' concept of learning)

- experience difficulty in making connections and linking ideas

- be passive (*'Show me what it's all about'*, *'Go on, impress me'*, *'Where are the handouts for this?'*)

- see learning as a means to an end (extrinsic motivation).

Deep learners tend to:

- look for meaning

- want an active interaction with the subject matter

- link learning with life, and change attitudes and beliefs when assimilating new information

- relate new information to previous knowledge (build structures)

- examine evidence carefully and use it critically

- have an interest in learning for its own sake (intrinsic motivation).

While the characteristics of the deep learner look more attractive, we often need to function as surface learners in order to be successful in a system dominated by assessment and examinations. Teachers would be neglecting their duties if they did not conscientiously prepare learners for examinations. Indeed, surface learning is a necessary stage on the way to deep learning. However, if we want to develop learners who can transfer their skills from one context to another, then it is deep learning we should be encouraging. This is quite apart from the dividend of personal development that deep learning brings.

WHAT CAN TEACHERS DO?

The challenge is to encourage deep learning as the general rule while limiting surface learning to those occasions where it is specifically required.

What seems to matter most in making learning meaningful is the attitude of the teacher. For example, if the only justification a teacher can find for learning is that, *'You'll need it for the exam,'* then the chances of developing a deep approach are remote. Fortunately, there are some practical steps the teacher can take. For example:

1 Offer the learner control of the process when it is practical to do so. The teacher may have little control of the subject matter to be taught, but in certain circumstances, and under appropriate guidance, it may possible to offer learners control over how much time is devoted to certain topics or the sequence in which they are studied.

2 Make it possible for learners to use different study methods. We can all call to mind learners who prefer to learn by sitting in a library and reading a book, and those who need to talk ideas through with others. Most teachers intuitively know that learning is not monolithic and vary their tactics to accommodate the needs of the learners and the subject matter being taught.

3 Differentiate learning in a way that avoids crude definitions of 'ability'. There are many ways of differentiating learning.

One of the key terms here seems to be 'variety'. Unfortunately, it takes a great deal of time and effort to develop appropriate materials and plan for using a range of techniques. It may be in this area that teachers need the greatest support.

Learning strategies

Research by Peter Honey and Alan Mumford suggests that learners have four basic learning strategies:

- **theorists** are believers in systems; they are logical, objective, like to think things through analytically; they are perfectionists

- **reflectors** chew things over; they are thoughtful, creative, good listeners, and frequently adopt a low profile

- **activists** jump in at the deep end; they are enthusiastic, and look for new challenges

- **pragmatists** enjoy experimenting with new ideas; they are practical, problem solvers.

(From P. Honey and A. Mumford, *The Manual of Learning Styles*, self-published, 1986.)

Although each of us uses a blend of strategies, and the emphasis may change over a period of time, understanding of our own preferred strategy can be very useful. For example, in some academic subjects, one learning strategy may be more appropriate than another while a blend of strategies may be needed to achieve success in certain jobs. This is why business and commerce place such emphasis on forming balanced teams for problem solving. The most successful teams are not necessarily those composed of individuals with virtuoso talent.

Stop and think: Can you recognise different learning strategies?
Try allocating each of the learning strategies to the original *Star Trek* officers Kirk, Spock, 'Bones' and Scotty. How do the scriptwriters use different talents to complement each other?

Comment
Presumably, Gene Roddenbury, the creator of Star Trek, *had no knowledge of the work of Honey and Mumford, but he seems to have known instinctively how to create a balanced team. Kirk is the activist, Spock is the theorist, Scotty is the pragmatist and 'Bones' is the reflector.*

For the individual learner, the point is not to identify a learning strategy as one's own and see it as immutable. An understanding of learning strategies should be used to develop a flexibility of response – a capacity to select and use any particular learning strategy when it is appropriate.

For the teacher, an understanding of learning strategies can point the way to more coherent planning, and help avoid having to provide a medley of methods in the vague hope that one or the other will hit the target. Additionally, a knowledge of students' preferred learning strategies should influence the formation of groups. If a teacher allows groupings based on similar learning strategies:

- the theorists will ask for clearer guidelines if a task is open-ended, complain about a lack of suitable evidence to work on and not be satisfied unless they can find a perfect solution

- the reflectors will spend endless amounts of time in discussion, but have great difficulty in presenting their group's findings

- the activists will compete with each other for leadership, quickly become bored with the task and look for new stimulation

- the pragmatists will rapidly lose patience with having no practical problems to resolve, become bored and question how what they are doing relates to 'real' life.

WHAT CAN TEACHERS DO?

1 Clearly, the accurate identification of preferred learning strategies can lead to more effective group formation that mixes the individuals, but rotates the roles so that everyone has to take the lead, record the findings, gather the evidence and report the conclusions. Teachers have a clear justification for using structured *and* unstructured activities; putting the emphasis on emotion *and* rationality; mixing certainty *and* ambiguity; requiring answers under pressure of time *and* allowing for leisurely reflection.

2 However, in one respect we should be wary of introducing learners to the concept of learning strategies in an explicit way: it is common for the knowledge to be used to excuse failure ('*No wonder I don't get on at school – they don't address my learning strategy!*').

3 The challenge is to provide varied learning opportunities, which draw different styles into play (see Table 1.1).

4 Remember that it is not sufficient simply to discover a learning strategy and regard it as immutable. The point is to work with individuals to encourage a better all-round profile, increasing their repertoire of skills. If you find that certain learners heavily favour a theorist learning strategy, encourage them into activities that you know are appropriate to activists, reflectors and pragmatists.

Table 1.1 Activities best suited to each preferred learning strategy

	Students using this learning strategy learn best from:	To encourage this learning strategy teachers can:
Theorists	structured activities that follow a logical sequence with a clear purpose lectures, demonstrations, coaching rational analysis that leads to logical outcomes	encourage accuracy of recall give opportunities to work alone set clear goals using action planning call for logical, analytical thinking based on the collection of data use the learner's own special interests
Reflectors	activities that enable them to observe and think things over researching a subject and assembling data before being asked to act individual or group tasks that involve an exchange of views within a structured setting	ask open-ended questions which require reflection on processes and outcomes use paired and group work for reflection and observation set tasks that have more than one solution ask learners to draw on their own experience value creative and imaginative work
Activists	group work, role-play, challenging games unstructured activities that emphasise the excitement and drama of new ideas opportunities for them to take the lead	create situations where individuals learn from mistakes create situations in which taking risks is acceptable value initiative and independence give credit for intuition and 'gut' feelings that may not be logically sound encourage learners to approach tasks in a variety of different ways
Pragmatists	practical demonstrations, coaching, simulations, work-experience, project work trying things out group or individual work involving action planning and project work	set clear goals indicate a practical context or relevance for the work learners are doing value thoroughness, systematic note-taking, skill acquisition offer opportunities to work alone encourage planning

Learning channels

Modern languages teachers will immediately recognise this hierarchy of skills:

- listening
- speaking
- reading
- writing

What is explicit in language learning is often implicit in other areas. For example, a topic in science may be introduced by listening to an explanation, developed through questioning and reading a textbook, and then reinforced by writing up an account of an experiment.

To these four primary learning channels we might add 'watching', since the use of video and CD-ROM is now widespread and most practical subjects will expect learners to master skills by observing a demonstration and then practising, or 'doing', them under supervision.

Unfortunately, teachers frequently limit their delivery by relying on a lecturing style alone. The full potential of the other learning channels is then lost. The list below gives an idea of the relative potencies of the learning channels.

It may be that we learn:

- 10% of what we read
- 20% of what we hear
- 30% of what we see
- 50% of what we both see and hear
- 70% of what we discuss with others
- 80% of what we experience personally
- 95% of what we teach.

This last figure will come as no surprise to teachers, who will know that *'In order to learn a subject well, you must teach it'*.

WHAT CAN TEACHERS DO?

1 Learning can be enhanced by paying attention to the different channels and ensuring that each one is activated in the course of a lesson. It may be helpful to link specific channels to the stages of a lesson. For example:

- introduction – listening/reading
- development – speaking/reading/writing/watching
- conclusion – doing (that is, practising skills)

2 Since some subjects depend more than others on the specific use of certain learning channels, it makes sense to learn from the experience of teachers in those subjects. For example, if you have the opportunity:

- observe the dynamic use of listening skills in modern languages (frequently using rhythm and repetition to reinforce learning)
- watch how teachers in technology subjects and physical education organise for practical activities (for example, *'I want you to come around this bench for a demonstration. I want you to form a semi-circle which starts here with Kathy and goes around to end with John. No-one will be standing behind anyone else. OK, let's move.'*)
- discuss with English teachers how they use marking to stimulate deeper thought (particularly the use of open-ended questions)
- look out for any classroom that has an unusual layout of desks and ask the teacher involved why they have chosen to use that arrangement.

Stop and think: Where are you now?
You may already be familiar with some or all of the aspects of learning discussed above. Your understanding of learning attitudes, styles and channels may be unconscious and intuitive or an explicit characteristic of your approach to teaching. But where are the gaps in your expertise?

Think back over your last two or three weeks of teaching. Can you identify specific occasions where you:
- encouraged deep approaches to learning?
- took account of preferred learning strategies?
- employed all the learning channels?

Summarise which areas you would like to develop further. How are you going to bring about the developments you desire?

Learning as a journey

If an individual's preferences on the three dimensions of learning attitude, strategy and channel were measured, it would provide a snapshot of where she was *at a particular moment*. The missing component would be any element that could explain the *dynamic* nature of learning. Research on the brain has shown that it is plastic: it will expand when praised and visibly shrink when subjected to sarcasm. In other words, the brain is not fixed; there is a physical response to external stimuli. Therefore, we need some explanation of the individual's experience as a learner, as that experience unfolds over time.

The model proposed in this book suggests a fourth dimension of learning, which augments the three described above and helps to explain how learning happens over time. This is the **Learner's Journey**. The ten steps of the Learner's Journey are adapted from Joseph Campbell's *The Hero with a Thousand Faces* and, more specifically, from Chris Vogler's *The Writer's Journey*, and are described on pages 23 to 26.

Vogler's work analyses the role of the hero as the focal point of various kinds of narrative. He suggests that, whether a hero embarks on an actual physical journey or not, he will typically undertake a quest, which will require survival through a number of physical and mental tests in order to seize a reward. The learner, like the hero, undertakes a hazardous, eventful and potentially rewarding journey, the final goal of which is the gaining of understanding and knowledge.

As an editor at Disney Studios, Vogler developed techniques to analyse scripts and predict which would become successful films. Based on previous work on myth and legend, Vogler's technique offered a powerful tool for explaining the success of films ranging from *The Wizard of Oz* to *Star Wars*. The challenge then was to see whether new scripts could be structured in order to aspire to the same mythic status. This did not mean that stories could be written to a formula that would guarantee success. The trick was to create variations on the theme, which interpreted the structures in new ways for different times and circumstances. Recent films influenced by this thinking include *Beauty and the Beast*, *Aladdin* and *The Lion King*.

Archetypes

Before considering the journey itself and the role of the hero, it is worth pausing to reflect on some of the archetypes that the hero – or the learner – will encounter along the way. Some of these will exert a positive influence, while others will appear to be negative. However, even threatening archetypes can be beneficial if the hero of the story overcomes them in struggling to reach a goal.

In the classroom, the teacher will undertake a variety of roles in her interactions with each learner, which are strongly reflected in the archetypes identified by Vogler and described below. The ability to move smoothly between these roles is part of the art of teaching. If a teacher fails to communicate why she has to switch between 'mentor', 'herald' and 'threshold guardian', for example, or even shirks one of these roles, the result may be difficulties in forming productive relationships with learners.

Mentor

The most important archetype that the teacher embodies is the **mentor**. In myth and legend, mentors are usually positive figures. In the classroom, they should always be so. The word itself originates from *The Odyssey* where Mentor was left to guide Telemachus while Odysseus was fighting in the Trojan Wars. Mentors may act out the role of guide, conscience or trainer to the hero.

Mentors do not necessarily befriend the hero. They can be demanding, argumentative and difficult, even abrasive, but they always act in the best interests of the hero. In some narratives, they die in furthering the cause of the hero. The mentor may have undergone the same, or similar, ordeals as the hero is about to experience and be able to offer gifts that can help the hero on the journey. The best mentors ensure that the gifts are earned and that, as the hero progresses, he develops his own inner guide, which makes the original mentor redundant.

There are films that portray teachers directly as both mentor and hero – from Robert Donat as Mr Chips (*Goodbye Mr Chips*) to Richard Dreyfuss as Mr Holland (*Mr Holland's Opus*).

Herald

The **herald** issues the challenge, inviting the hero to engage in development and change. He is often unwelcome and his message is frequently resisted. However, he also brings news of opportunities and the hero usually acknowledges that the time has come to move on. The role of the herald is often combined with that of mentor.

Threshold guardian

The **threshold guardian** tests the hero's resolve. Although she is frequently seen as being negative, particularly because she limits the hero's freedom to act, she can become an ally. Typical teacher roles as a threshold guardian include examiner, disciplinarian, corridor supervisor and resource controller.

Shadow

The **shadow** represents a dark energy. He may be an outright villain or an antagonist. Once again, his function is to challenge the hero, to test her resolve. Many learners perceive their teacher, or any other authority figure, as a shadow. Shadows are frequently charismatic, energetic and may represent the other side of the hero's personality.

Shapeshifter

Over a year or even a few weeks, a teacher may fulfil all of the roles outlined above, sometimes combining them in any single lesson or encounter with a learner. Therefore, teachers should be aware that they may also seem to fulfil the role of 'shapeshifter' to students. The **shapeshifter** is unpredictable and frequently dangerous, but is often a catalyst for change. Fellow learners are more likely to be seen in this role than as mentors, threshold guardians or shadows.

Trickster

The **trickster's** role is to cut the hero down to size. She acts as a clown, provoking laughter, frequently having the last word and providing comic relief. In schools, this role is more likely to be taken by another learner rather than by the teacher.

Hero

The most important of the archetypes is that of the **hero**. The word 'hero' comes from a Greek root meaning 'to protect and to serve'. The role is connected with ideas of action (the hero takes risks), self-sacrifice (which may involve death, but the hero may simply sacrifice an old way of thinking or behaving), and growth (the hero is expected to achieve new knowledge and self-awareness). Each hero is a unique combination of these elements.

Clearly, teachers may be seen as heroes on their own journey, but the emphasis here is on the teacher as a supporting character, rather than in the role of hero.

The Hero's Journey

Set out below is an outline of Vogler's twelve steps of the Hero's Journey. The steps are explored using references to *Hamlet* and the science fiction film *The Matrix*. Remember that for any particular narrative the steps may not occur in the order given here, and some may appear to be omitted completely, but the basic pattern continues to emerge regardless of genre, period or style.

1 Ordinary world

The starting point for the journey is the day-to-day world inhabited by the hero of the story. He may already be remarkable in some way, but the omens begin to gather and indicate that he is about to engage in radical change.

Hamlet
After the death of his father and the hasty re-marriage of his mother, Prince Hamlet feels embittered and resentful. When we are first introduced to him, there is no focus for these feelings.

The Matrix

In *The Matrix*, Neo lives two lives. Agent Smith (Neo's shadow) points out to him that *'in one you are a program writer for a respectable software company ... the other is lived in computers ... where you have committed every computer crime we have a law for'*.

2   Call to action

The 'call to action' is an invitation to undertake an adventure. In some stories, the hero has little choice about whether to accept. For example, she may have to undertake a series of tests to reach a desired goal.

Hamlet

With the help of an ally, Horatio, Hamlet encounters the ghost of his father, who reveals the truth about his murder. The ghost calls for revenge, which Hamlet agrees to fulfil. From now on, any action that does not lead to revenge causes Hamlet distress.

The Matrix

Neo receives messages from the mysterious Morpheus (his mentor) on the Internet, and meets Trinity, another key character. Neo is uncomfortable in his current world, but is at a loss to know what to do about his unease.

3   Refusal of the call

The first response to the call to action is often one of reluctance. The hero may refuse to leave the comfort of the known world. He may fear failure, be reluctant to make the necessary commitment, or simply be concerned about what someone else might think.

Hamlet

Self-doubt begins to set in. Can Hamlet really trust the word of a ghost? What further proof could he find to verify the suspicion of murder?

The Matrix

Neo is pursued by Agents, but refuses to follow Morpheus' advice and falls into their hands. After a harrowing ordeal he is released, but believes he is waking up from a dream.

4   Meeting the mentor and finding the talisman

The mentor is a central figure in the individual's quest. He provides essential support in engaging the hero in the quest. The mentor may provide a talisman, which has a role to play in guiding the hero. It may be anything ranging from a weapon to a piece of advice or a set of rules.

Hamlet
Hamlet has a number of mentors, who point the way towards action. First, the ghost reveals the truth; later the player king graphically demonstrates how he should be behaving; while even Yorick, the dead jester, has a lesson to teach.

The Matrix
Eventually, Neo meets his mentor, the legendary Morpheus, who tells him about the 'splinter in his mind' that is driving Neo's actions.

5   Crossing the threshold

The individual finally makes a commitment to enter the new world, where different rules apply. One factor that may bring about the decision to 'cross the threshold' is a vision of what the hero could become, which is attractive or meaningful. Alternatively, the hero may have no choice and be driven to cross the threshold by the actions of others or a desire for revenge.

Hamlet
As a temporary measure, Hamlet pretends to be mad in order to cover his actions until he can satisfy himself about the truth of his father's death. He makes up his own rules about how to conduct himself in this world.

The Matrix
Morpheus offers Neo a choice of a red or a blue pill. The blue one will return Neo to the Matrix and to the world he already knows; the red one will lead to the truth. Neo chooses the red pill.

6   Trials, rewards, enemies and friends

The main part of the journey begins and we soon begin to identify with the hero, who overcomes every trial.

Hamlet
Hamlet encounters Rosencrantz and Guildenstern (tricksters and shapeshifters), has a traumatic interview with his mother, kills Polonius and meets the players.

The Matrix
Having taken the pill and been released from the Matrix (his 'old world'), Neo meets others who know the truth, and begins his training. The Agents are specifically identified as the threshold guardians and later we discover that Cypher, an apparent ally, is in fact a trickster who betrays the trust of Morpheus and the others.

7   Approaching the inmost cave

The hero begins to prepare for the final stage of the journey.

Hamlet
Hamlet finally hits on a plan to confirm the ghost's accusation. With the help of the players, Hamlet prepares to stage *The Murder of Gonzago*.

The Matrix
Morpheus is captured and held in a top security building. Neo sets out to rescue him with Trinity.

8   Supreme ordeal

The hero reaches the final trial and prepares to seize the reward. The hero may use weapons picked up on the journey.

Hamlet
Claudius' guilty reaction to the play removes all doubts from Hamlet's mind. But Claudius is now fully aware that Hamlet knows the truth about the King's murder and plots to get rid of him. He decides to send his troublesome nephew to England, where his death has been arranged.

The Matrix
Neo and Trinity attack the building in which Morpheus is being held. Neo begins to realise his potential and challenges an Agent. Even though he does not win, he grows in strength. Trinity is astonished at his ability to move as quickly as an Agent.

9   The reward

The hero achieves the prize, which may be an object or something more abstract such as self-knowledge.

Hamlet
Hamlet's reward after staging *The Murder of Gonzago* is certainty about the murder of his father. The play has the side-effect of pricking Gertrude's conscience.

The Matrix
Neo saves Morpheus and Trinity and they retreat from danger to Morpheus' ship.

10 The road back

The dark forces re-group as the hero attempts to return with the reward.

Hamlet

Hamlet is sent to England where his death has been arranged. However, he defeats the forces ranged against him. Hamlet returns to Denmark, only to hear the news of Ophelia's death.

The Matrix

After another encounter with Agent Smith, Neo attempts to exit the Matrix, but is shot. He appears to die.

11 Resurrection

From the experiences of the journey, a new person emerges. The death may be literal or symbolic.

Hamlet

Hamlet's resurrection occurs as he is returning from the journey to England, and in a very literal way. After his soliloquy to Yorick, he sees Ophelia's funeral cortège. After

Laertes has made his speech about his sister, Hamlet jumps into Ophelia's grave and grapples with Laertes, thereby setting in motion the plot line that will lead to his own death at the fencing tournament. Later, in combat with Laertes, Hamlet is stabbed but manages to take the poisoned sword and uses it to kill Laertes and Claudius.

The Matrix

Neo's resurrection is literal too. Shot by Agent Smith and with enemies closing in, Neo is called back to life by the love of Trinity who reveals that Neo must be 'the one' they have been searching for. Neo returns to life with renewed strength, defeats the Agents and sees the Matrix for what it really is.

12 Return with the elixir

Not only is the reward achieved and the challenge successfully completed but the extent of the hero's success is recognised by others. The next journey begins.

Hamlet
By the end of the play, Hamlet is purged of his responsibility to the ghost of his father and Denmark is a country freed from corruption. All his enemies are now dead. Horatio agrees that he will tell the true story of why Hamlet acted as he did. Hamlet dies knowing that his reputation will survive his death.

The Matrix
In a closing telephone conversation, Neo explains, '*I don't know the future. I didn't come here to tell you how this is going to end, only how it's going to begin. Where we go from here is up to you.*'

> **Stop and think: Do the twelve steps of the Hero's Journey make sense to you?**
> Think of any narrative that you know well. Does the same pattern emerge?
> What are the variations? How do the archetypes show themselves?

The Learner's Journey

Vogler's work on narrative structure offers us a number of possibilities for thinking about learning and suggests techniques for supporting the learning process. For example, if we agree that the learner is the 'hero' of her own story, undergoing similar trials, we should ask ourselves how we as teachers can operate more effectively as mentors.

The journey structure may offer us a way of predicting when to make interventions, perhaps forecasting periods of greatest stress. However, while we may be able to use the journey as a guide ourselves, it may be unwise to make the metaphor explicit to learners. The Learner's Journey is largely an inward one of individual growth and discovery. This is a rather abstract concept for younger learners to appreciate and difficult to communicate effectively. After all, the journey has to be lived, not discussed.

The description of each of the steps of the Learner's Journey set out below is followed by key questions, which point the way to the more detailed explanations advanced in the coming Sections.

1 Ordinary world (Section Two)

The adventure begins in the world that the learner inhabits before the 'call to action'. For teachers in schools, the ordinary world of the learners will be dominated by family and friends. Teachers frequently make inaccurate assumptions about learners' backgrounds. In addition, the school itself assumes the form of an ordinary world.

- How can teachers acquire and use knowledge of the learner's ordinary world?
- How can such knowledge help teachers to plan learning programmes and anticipate obstacles?
- What are the factors currently affecting the ordinary world of the school?

2 The learning impulse (Section Three)

In one way, children in schools do not have the option of choosing not to accept the 'call to action', since they *have* to attend school and the lessons devised for them. However, even though children attend lessons, there may be a refusal to act on the natural impulse to learn while they are there.

- How can teachers help learners to develop a personal vision that will sustain them through inevitable periods of self-doubt and anxiety?
- How can teachers use learning objectives to sustain that vision?

3 Meeting the mentor (Section Four)

The learner encounters a key mentor in the shape of the teacher. However, other support may come from friends, relatives or role models.

- What exactly do mentors do? How can their expertise be developed and their role enhanced?

4 Crossing the threshold (Section Five)

The learner enters the new world and begins the quest. The new world may be represented by transfer between Primary and Secondary school, encountering a new teacher for the first time or simply attending the next lesson. In each case, there is a threshold to be crossed.

- What models are available to help teachers understand the process of change that is ushered in when learners 'cross the threshold'?
- How can initial success be maintained?
- How can teachers reconcile the many different roles that they are asked to play (mentor, herald, threshold guardian) in meeting learners' needs?

5 Trials and errors (Section Six)

On their adventure, most learners will:

- meet new people
- experience fear of failure
- encounter problems in keeping up with the work
- endure feelings of inadequacy
- experience the thrill of mastering new skills
- learn to tolerate pressure.

If, on balance, the learner has more positive than negative experiences, he will probably emerge as an effective learner, capable of operating with some degree of autonomy.

- How can the teacher anticipate the difficulties and provide appropriate support in the learner's encounters?
- How can teachers avoid a failure being turned into a relapse, which might cement unproductive attitudes?

---

6 Allies and enemies (Section Seven)

Teaching staff, relatives and friends act in the role of ally to the learner. However, they may pose threats as well as offering support. In addition, learning resources may provide support in the guise of a talisman.

- Who (or what) are the allies of the learner?
- What methods can the teacher use to promote co-learners as allies?

---

7 Tests and examinations (Section Eight)

This step is equivalent to 'the supreme ordeal' in the hero's journey. The ordeal may take the form of short tests, preparation for exams, examinations themselves or the development of a portfolio of work.

- How can teachers maximise this stage for personal development as well as the achievement of qualifications?
- How can the individual be encouraged to continue aspiring to deep learning when everything seems to point to the centrality of the surface approach?

---

8 Reward and recognition (Section Nine)

Rewards may come in the form of external qualifications or a sense of achievement and personal growth on completing the programme.

● Is there a difference between reward and recognition?
● How can we use both to reinforce learning and celebrate success in all its forms?

---

9 A new beginning (Section Ten)

The new beginning for learners involves stepping forward into the excitement of the next journey. Their confidence will be determined partly by the 'elixir' of qualifications, which validates their last adventure, but also by their self-assurance, which may have nothing to do with any formal qualifications achieved. For teachers, this step represents an opportunity to reflect on the lessons learned from the last generations of learners and use them to animate the next.

● How can teachers audit their practice to improve the quality of teaching and learning?

---

10 Closure (Section Eleven)

The learners' perception of the 'ordinary world' is now transformed as a result of the journey. The challenge is how to integrate their new selves into the transformed reality.

● How can learners use the lessons of the journey to make their way in the ordinary world?
● What are the challenges that will face them in the rapidly changing world of work?

A Learning Framework (Section Twelve)

Most teachers will see how the ten steps outlined above could apply to a school career or even a year of learning, but what about the module of work or the individual lesson? This question is considered throughout the book, but examined in detail in the final Section.

● How can the ten steps of the Learner's Journey be built into learning programmes?
● What is the minimum and maximum that can be achieved in an individual lesson?

Stop and think: At what levels does the concept of the Learner's Journey apply?
Would you apply the concept of the journey only to the macro-level of the whole school career? For example, does it begin with transfer from Primary education and end with GCSE? What about the micro-level of the term, the unit of work or even the single lesson?

Comment
If we view each person as a hero, on her way to fulfilling a destiny, then having a structural map of her experiences might help us to predict when to make interventions to help her finish her learning programme. For example, how could we enhance the natural impulse to learn so that fewer refuse (either physically or mentally) to participate, or provide an improved environment for those who have refused in the past? How could we then help students in 'crossing the threshold'?

Further, the teacher needs to participate in the journey too. This should not merely be a vicarious involvement – it should be recognised that the teacher is also on a journey and that interaction with a learner may have an effect on the teacher, just as the teacher affects the learner.

By presenting the learning programme as a structured experience, teachers could help learners to understand the processes they are going through. This is particularly useful when difficulties arise. However, this should not be taken literally with learners being told that they are 'on a journey with ten steps'. The use of anecdotes about successful individuals who have undertaken a programme, overcome the difficulties and won through is far more effective.

This book is particularly concerned with building confidence, raising self-esteem and developing individual autonomy. Learning is a dynamic process, which changes those who engage in it. Our quest, as teachers, is to find an answer to the question '*How can we make the learning experience better for learners?*'

Arrangement of the Sections

Sections Two to Eleven begin with a brief explanation of how the steps of the Hero's Journey are adapted to those of the Learner's Journey, under the heading *Background*. A detailed exposition follows, under *Application*, interspersed with questions designed to stimulate further thinking (*Stop and think*) and suggestions for classroom applications (*What can teachers do?*). The final Section suggests how the steps of the journey can be used to structure learning at a variety of levels.

SUMMARY

◆ CURRENT MODELS OF LEARNING OFFER ONLY A LIMITED VIEW OF THE EXPERIENCE OF LEARNERS.

◆ THE HERO'S JOURNEY OFFERS A PARALLEL TO THE QUEST FOR KNOWLEDGE THAT A LEARNER UNDERTAKES.

◆ THE LEARNER'S JOUNREY CAN BE BROKEN DOWN INTO STAGES THAT CAN HELP TO INFORM CLASSROOM PRACTICE.

◆ TEACHERS PLAY A NUMBER OF ROLES IN SUPPORTING LEARNERS ON THEIR JOURNEYS.

Ordinary world

In Section Two we learn that:

● Schools can create an appropriate environment for learning.

● 'Continuing professional development' is a powerful tool for promoting learning.

● This book can support teachers considering the performance threshold assessment.

BACKGROUND

The 'ordinary world' of the hero frames the quest. It is here that the challenge is initially thrown down and, in most cases, it is to a transformed ordinary world that the hero will return (see Section Eleven). The 'transformation' may affect either the hero, the ordinary world or both, but the key to the quest is change.

The movement of the journey is a familiar one: from the everyday to the extraordinary world of discovery; from the known to the unknown. For the audience, the path may appear to be well-trodden, at least in its general outline, but for the hero this is new and uncharted territory.

The ordinary world may be stultifying and inhibiting. The hero may be restless and keen for the excitement of the new. On the other hand, the hero may only reluctantly be considering change, experiencing the powerful undertow of the known world too strongly to break away easily. Perhaps the hero has responsibilities that cannot easily be disregarded. We recognise the reluctant hero just as readily as the buccaneering adventurer.

In some narratives, the ordinary world is established in a prologue. Shakespeare summarises the ordinary worlds of *Romeo and Juliet* and *Henry V* in this way. Generally, however, he uses the more naturalistic device of introducing characters who stroll onto the stage in conversation to set the scene that we are about to encounter.

For Luke Skywalker in *Star Wars*, the ordinary world is the farm of his aunt and uncle. He feels constrained and frustrated but can see no immediate way out of the dullness he perceives all around him. Macbeth, like the Roman general Maximus in the film *Gladiator*, is a loyal soldier, recently involved in a successful campaign against the enemies of his country. Unlike Luke Skywalker, Macbeth and Maximus are already exceptional figures in their own worlds. But Macbeth is about to be touched by unknown and unknowable forces, which will propel him into a world of treachery, deceit and murder. Maximus' world is not dominated by the supernatural, but he too will experience the consequences of the murder of a king and undergo a long and complex journey ending in his own death.

APPLICATION

Learners may occupy a number of ordinary worlds. The most obvious is the home from which they travel to school every day, but Primary school is also an 'ordinary world' in the adventure of progressing into Secondary education. In addition, there is the background noise of the wider ordinary world that they recognise, but understand in only the vaguest way. This is the world of work and adult activity. Most children are keen to progress into this world as quickly as possible, but recognise that they must undergo the apprenticeship of school.

Stop and think: How well do you know your learners' ordinary worlds?

Your local library will have census information that can tell you a lot about the ordinary world of your learners. Try consulting it to find answers to questions such as those below.

- What is the typical skill level of parents in your catchment area? Unskilled? Semi-skilled? Professional?
- What proportions of families are in social classes A, B, C and D?
- What is the age profile of families?
- How many single parent families are there?
- What is the ethnic mix in the community as a whole? Is it reflected in your school?

Comment

Information like this is helpful in understanding the backgrounds of your learners. However, the remainder of this Section moves the focus away from direct consideration of individual learners and concerns itself with aspects of the ordinary world of the school.

Adventures in Learning

In common with most other social institutions, schools have been subjected to considerable change and development in recent decades. This has created an atmosphere unknown to previous generations of learners. Set out below is a brief consideration of four areas of development that may have a profound effect on schools and teachers:

1   learning organisations

2   conducive learning environment

3   continuing professional development

4   performance threshold assessment.

Learning organisations

There is increasing interest in the concept of the 'learning organisation'. This has been defined as:

> ... an organisation that facilitates the learning of all its members and continuously transforms itself.

from *The Learning Company* by M. Pedler, J. Burgoyne and T. Boydell, (McGraw Hill, 1991)

Schools should exemplify the learning organisation concept since learning is their core business, yet frequently this is not the case. The paradox is a common one in other sectors too. We often seem to read about financial advisers who go bankrupt; care institutions that become centres of abuse; safety organisations that are prosecuted for failing to observe the most basic regulations. It sometimes appears that organisations become so involved in delivering their service that they fail to practise what they preach.

What does a learning organisation 'look like'? The characteristics outlined below are adapted from those suggested in *The Learning Company*.

1   Participative policy making

Schools have a very wide range of stakeholders including learners, teachers, parents, governors and the local community. All of these should be invited to take part in discussions about policy. This should involve a recognition that tensions and conflicts will occur, along with a commitment to resolving them or working them through to a consensus.

2   The learning approach to strategy

Policies are decided on a provisional basis. Opportunities for revising policies are built into a system of constant review and analysis. The views of people who have to implement policy are sought and valued.

3 Using information and communication technology (ICT)

This refers to the use of ICT to inform and empower people. It also refers to the access that people within the organisation have to information.

4 Internal exchange

Those who work within the organisation should view themselves as suppliers with internal customer needs to satisfy. Indeed, the aim should be to go beyond 'satisfaction' to 'customer delight'. This should be complemented by an atmosphere of co-operation and an appreciation of the framework of the needs of the organisation as a whole. Schools have a wide range of 'customers', both internal and external.

5 Enabling structures

Departments and individual roles are blurred as the internal structures respond flexibly to the need for change. Such flexibility promotes a creative openness to internal and external pressures.

6 Self-development opportunities for all

The resources of the organisation for self-development are equitably distributed and accessible to all. Individuals are encouraged to take responsibility for their own development.

Stop and think: Your school as a learning organisation
Do the criteria fit your school? Would you describe it as a 'learning organisation'? Perhaps some of the characteristics are in place, but not others. Which are they? It is rare to find schools with a genuine customer orientation.

What responsibility will you take for creating organisational change and development that will bring a learning organisation into being?

Comment
Learners have a right to expect a certain standard of service from their school. However, rights are rarely explored explicitly with children. Responsibilities, on the other hand, will almost certainly be embodied in a set of rules or policies, which cover everything from lateness and uniform to coursework and examination entries.

This situation in schools reverses the picture to be found in society as a whole, where there is a widespread belief that our emphasis may have swung too far towards rights and neglected the importance of personal responsibility. For example, we frequently hear complaints about the length of time that patients sometimes have to wait for hospital appointments and treatment, but how often do we hear of apologies for the thousands of appointments for which patients do not turn up, wasting millions of pounds?

WHAT CAN TEACHERS DO?

1 In discussion with learners, balance aspects of rights and responsibilities. Produce a 'learners' charter', which sets out what you (the teacher) and the school will do, and suggest that your group should create a draft 'learners' obligation' using a similar format. For example, a 'learner's charter' might include promises from the teacher to:

- provide the necessary learning resources

- mark and return work within a specified period

- whenever possible, take learner preferences into account when planning work.

You might then agree that learners should make every effort to:

- arrive on time

- always have the appropriate materials and equipment for lessons

- meet assessment deadlines for coursework, and so on.

2 You may prefer to customise the 'charter' and 'obligations' documents to reflect your learners and your classroom situation.

3 There are various examples of 'charter' that you could use as models. For example, your local hospital will almost certainly have a patients' charter. It is worth making a collection of these, to examine whether there is any attempt to balance rights and responsibilities.

Conducive learning environment

Most teachers tend to think of the learning environment as referring only to the room in which they work. This is understandable, since there is often little that can be done about the shape and design of a whole building. However, the best organisations make every effort to overcome the limitations of their working space. They know that there is only one chance to make a good first impression.

Stop and think: What model of learning is suggested by your school and classroom?
Analyse the design features that make many business reception areas smart and welcoming. Try applying the same bench marks to your classroom and school. If you find a discrepancy, how could you bring about changes?

Should the same criteria be applied to corridors and toilets, as to classrooms?

What could you use as a model? In other words, thinking about interior design, which rooms in other buildings would you most like your classroom and school to resemble?

Comment
Your model for an attractive interior may have been your home, one of the great country houses, a civic building such as an art gallery or the offices of an international

---

corporation. In school, it may be impossible to achieve such a 'look' in its entirety, but what would a good approximation look like?

Going for a quick-fix in re-modelling the learning environment may not be possible, or even desirable, but what about a three year plan to introduce carefully thought out use of plants and pictures, for example?

What unconscious model is revealed by the layout of your classroom? If the room in which you are asking students to work is austere and unwelcoming, how might that affect learning?

'Atmosphere' is much less tangible than the physical environment, but probably even more important for learning. It depends largely on the attitude of the teacher. If the teacher is committed and enthusiastic, then most of the learners will be similarly engaged.

WHAT CAN TEACHERS DO?

Teachers can create the right psychological climate by, among other things:

1 learning and using the names of all group members at an early stage

2 valuing the knowledge that they already possess and consistently highlighting that learners are not blank slates

3 involving learners, wherever possible, in the process of learning (for example, can they exercise choice over the order in which subjects will be studied?).

Continuing professional development (CPD)

In recent years, a systematic approach to developing individuals known as 'continuing professional development' (CPD) has been growing in importance. Chris Senior, in an article in *Training and Development*, defined CPD as:

> … the systematic maintenance, improvement and broadening of knowledge and skills and the development of personal qualities for the execution of professional duties throughout working life.

Chris Senior, in *Training and Development*

In other words, learning and development should be activities that go on all the time, not just on courses.

Taking care of your career now means managing constant change. This is true whether you see yourself working in your current job for the foreseeable future or you expect to move on to something else quite soon. CPD can help you to keep your skills, knowledge and understanding up to date. With CPD you take personal responsibility for adapting to change.

The *aims* of the process are to:

- raise personal levels of achievement
- link personal development to organisational need
- attain local and national targets for lifelong learning.

The *benefits* for individual teachers are:

- improved skill levels
- higher motivation
- greater confidence in facing demands for flexibility in job roles
- improved job satisfaction.

This sounds very attractive, but as we all recognise the problem is finding the time for personal development, when there are so many other pressures that dominate your attention. It is all too easy to say 'yes' to immediate demands and forget about the longer-term investment needed for learning and development.

Taking one word at a time, CPD may be defined as:

continuing	the process extends throughout a working life, and is not restricted to a specific period of time (whether a one day course or the years needed for a university degree)
professional	the process relates to the execution of specialist duties and aims to improve and broaden the knowledge, skills and (where appropriate) qualifications of the individual
development	the process is systematic and progressive in the enhancement of personal and professional qualities.

In some schools, CPD is already in place. However, if this is not the case, and you find the idea of taking personal control of your professional development attractive, the points set out below can provide a rationale and a practical programme of action that will help you to achieve your aims. The material for supporting your own CPD process can be implemented and reviewed on a yearly basis.

The benefits of CPD point to a series of *key issues*. In order for the process to be coherent and vigorous, it is important that it helps the individual to:

- **respond to change**

  CPD should be seen as a stimulating activity. This is much more than simply managing to cope with change. CPD should make it possible for teachers to anticipate change and respond positively.

- **appreciate the need for a personal investment in training**

  The world of work in general, and teaching in particular, is changing rapidly. Employers expect more of employees now, demanding greater individual autonomy. In the interests of the present and the future, individuals should consider giving higher priority to the investment of time in lifelong learning.

- **take ownership**

  People exhibit greater commitment if they are involved in their own development. The aim of these materials is to give teachers control over their own development process by recognising, creating and using the learning opportunities that occur in the course of their personal and working lives.

- **plan and focus on the future**

  Part of the CPD process involves the creation of a 'personal development plan' (PDP), which will provide a focus and a framework to:

  1   identify individual needs

  2   plan and implement learning activities

  3   record and review progress.

  The PDP may be the same document as an agreed statement and action plan from your school's appraisal process, if it has one.

- **reconcile a number of interests**

  The CPD process should take account of:

  1   personal aspirations

  2   professional needs

  3   your school's needs.

  These can only be reconciled through a process of open discussion between curriculum managers and the teacher. There may be a need to emphasise one element over another in a particular year, but over the long term there should be an equitable balance.

- **respond to learning opportunities**

  CPD should be built around quality learning opportunities relevant to individual needs and, where appropriate, should include qualifications. This implies that the individual should not only be thinking in terms of attending courses for professional development – there are many other opportunities available.

- **record progress**

  As part of the process, each individual should keep a log of learning experiences, which demonstrates how he has implemented the PDP. This could form part of an appraisal discussion, but it is also important for individuals to consider how far they have come and where they might go next, even without any links to appraisal.

- **obtain support**

  Managers at every level should provide support, guidance and mentoring for CPD. For most organisations, the formal review of progress will take place at the end of the appraisal cycle. However, informal discussion of progress is of great value when promoting CPD. The teacher working alone on CPD can still find the necessary support without linking in to any other management systems such as appraisal.

Most people find it helpful to work with a colleague on their CPD in order to get the best out of the process and themselves. Talking to colleagues may lead to a more realistic consideration of work and personal needs, stimulating the single-mindedness that is often necessary for successful CPD.

Stop and think: CPD in your organisation

Take a few minutes to reflect on the issues raised so far. Use the following questions as prompts, then add any further observations of your own.

- Which of the benefits of CPD indicated above are particularly important to you? Which of the key issues (coping with change, personal investment in training, and so on) are particularly important at the moment?
- Does your school have an appraisal process? How could appraisal and CPD complement each other?
- Are you considering implementing a CPD process as a personal project rather than in a whole-school context? If so, where will you find support?
- What might stand in the way of implementing CPD in your school? How might these difficulties be overcome?

Self-assessment

The first stage of any CPD process is to consider where you are now. If you have no previous involvement in CPD, this may involve a wide-ranging review of your career so far. After that, the review will cover the previous 12 months only.

Personal development plan

This sets out how you are going to develop yourself over the next year. Any targets set as part of your appraisal should be included in the plan. However, make sure that your development plan takes into account the needs of the school as well as your own.

Learning log

As you begin to implement your plan, it is important to record what you do and your thoughts and feelings about what happens. Another way of representing the process is by reference to a cycle of activities.

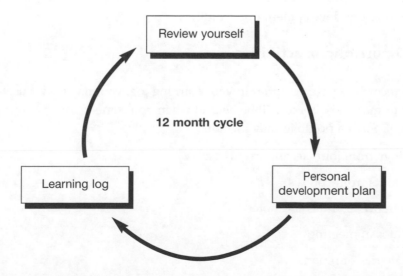

The time required for CPD

Most people will spend no more than about two hours in self-review and planning activities at the beginning of the process. An approximate guideline for the amount of time you should spend on your development activities is a minimum of 35 hours per year. For some people, the time spent may be less; for many it will be considerably more. If this seems like a lot to you, do not forget that it is spread over a year and that CPD brings into the foreground activities that you would not normally class as being learning opportunities.

What are typical learning opportunities?

CPD does not replace attending courses or conferences. These are part of the development process too. What it does is bring out other activities that might have gone unrecognised before, and build them into your personal development programme. The following could all be recorded in your learning log:

- attending courses, conferences, seminars
- taking a night school class (as a learner or as a teacher)
- reading books and journal articles
- observing the work of other teachers
- visiting other schools and organisations
- using 'chance' opportunities such as overhearing a radio programme containing material or ideas that you can adapt for use in your teaching
- regularly watching television or listening to radio programmes about your subject
- searching electronic media such as the Internet
- undertaking a longer course of study (for example, an Open University degree)
- preparing and delivering a presentation
- writing a strategy document
- taking on the responsibilities of someone off work.

Your activities should spread over a range of learning opportunities. In other words, it is not enough that you attended five conferences in a year averaging seven hours per day in order to reach 35 hours. Your learning log should demonstrate how you used a number of different development opportunities.

The CPD portfolio of activities

As well as recording your activities in your learning log, you may find it useful to keep a portfolio of materials. These will be helpful when you come to review your personal development. Such a portfolio may include:

- cuttings from journals and magazines
- handouts from courses
- conference agendas and notes
- minutes of meetings
- summaries of reports.

Documentation

Use the questions set out below to create your own CPD forms. (These materials for planning and recording your CPD all relate to one-year targets. You may want to think in the longer term. If this is the case, simply substitute the word 'three' or 'five' for 'one' where you see 'one-year targets'.)

Reviewing yourself

	Questions	Your responses
1	**a** What areas of your work have gone particularly well this year? Why?	
	b What could be done by yourself or others to build on your successes?	
	c Who are the people who have helped most and could help further in your work?	
	d How could you influence these people so that your success continues?	
2	**a** What areas of your work have not gone particularly well this year? Why?	
	b What could have been done by yourself or others to improve things?	
	c Who are the people involved in the less successful side of your work?	
	d How could you influence them so that performance is improved?	
3	Are there any other problems that you met over the last year?	
4	What would you identify as your major targets over the next year?	
5	Anything else you would wish to add?	

Personal development plan

From your consideration of the questions above, you should now have a clear picture of where you are and where you would like to go. The next step is to construct your personal development plan.

	Questions	Your responses
1	What area(s) of skill/experience would you like to develop over the next year?	
2	What training needs will this generate?	
3	How will you achieve your one-year targets?	
4	How will you find the time?	
5	How will you find the money?	
6	What method will you use to acquire the skills/experience?	
7	Do you need to make any changes to the way you work now to achieve your one-year targets?	

Log of learning experiences

This simple pro-forma is designed to help you to keep a record of the learning experiences you value over the course of a year. You should list the learning experiences in column one; make your own brief comments on the value of what you learned in column two; put the date of the learning experience in column three and estimate the time you devoted to the activity in column four.

1. Experiences	2. Comments	3. Date	4. Time
(courses, reading, and so on)			

Performance threshold assessment

The UK government's intention in introducing the performance threshold was to offer classroom teachers the opportunity to have their expertise recognised through higher pay. Progress onto the upper pay range will be determined by the quality of work in the classroom, not by the acceptance of additional responsibilities. There is considerable literature available to guide teachers through the process and reproducing it here is of little value. However, set out in Table 2.1 is guidance on how the material in this book may be relevant to the five areas of the performance threshold assessment.

Table 2.1

Areas of the performance threshold assessment	Section in this book/subject
1 Knowledge and understanding	Section Two/CPD
2 Teaching and assessment	Section Four/Mentoring in a one-to-one discussion Section Seven/Learning structures Section Nine/Reward and recognition Section Twelve/Learning design
3 Student progress	Section Eight/Tests and examinations Section Ten/Classroom audit
4 Wider professional effectiveness	Section Two/CPD
5 Professional characteristics	Section Three/Aims and objectives Section Four/Mentoring in a one-to-one discussion Section Six/Motivation Section Nine/Reward and recognition Section Seven/High definition teaching Section Four/Mentoring in a one-to-one discussion

Interestingly, the only Section that does not have a place in this list is Section Eleven, which deals with the world outside the school and the changing expectations that students can expect to encounter when they find their first job.

SUMMARY

- THE CONCEPT OF THE 'ORDINARY WORLD' APPLIES TO THE SCHOOL AS WELL AS THE HOME.

- SCHOOLS NEED TO ADOPT THE ATTITUDES OF A 'LEARNING ORGANISATION' AS PART OF THEIR DEVELOPMENT.

- CONTINUING PROFESSIONAL DEVELOPMENT CAN BE A TOOL ADAPTED FOR WHOLE-SCHOOL OR INDIVIDUAL USE.

The learning impulse

In Section Three we learn that:

● A personal vision can be a powerful tool to motivate personal development.

● A vision on its own is not enough – most people also need short-term objectives and targets.

BACKGROUND

This Section combines two of the steps in the Hero's Journey: the 'call to action' and 'refusal of the call'.

The 'call to action' may take many forms. It may be specific, perhaps with a herald making a formal announcement (for example, the Sheriff of Nottingham announced an archery competition to trap Robin Hood). Or it could be implied: for example, a power figure may set the hero a challenge that has to be overcome on the way to fame and fortune. In *Star Wars*, Luke Skywalker accidentally finds the plea for help from Princess Leia. He seeks out Obi-Wan Kenobi, the intended recipient of the message and begins to guess at the possibility of his own destiny, but refuses to take up the challenge because he claims he is needed at home. The call could instead be an accidental meeting (as in Alfred Hitchcock's *Strangers on a Train*, in which two travellers plot their wives' murders), an electric moment of realisation (as in *Romeo and Juliet*) or an inner need for fulfilment (such as Neo's 'splinter in the mind' in *The Matrix*).

Heroes are frequently reluctant to take up the challenge. They often need repeated coaxing, and may only respond when there is no other option. This is encouraging for teachers because reluctance to respond is a daily reality for many.

Threshold guardians may have a powerful influence at this stage. These may be individuals who point to the negative results of taking up the call (*'That's a waste of time, you don't want to do that'*), or to previous, negative experiences of the individual learner. Refusal of the call is a rejection of personal self-interest or social purpose, or of the individual's 'dream' of a better life. Continued refusal of the call often leads to disaster – as with Hamlet.

When a hero is willing to respond to the call to action, this is usually because she is responding to an inner need. Applying the concept of the willing hero to learners in school would lead us to those who are instinctively deep learners.

APPLICATION

The learning impulse represents a desire to grow and change. This appears to be instinctive for babies, but on reaching the Secondary phase, many learners appear to have lost their momentum. Teachers may be relieved to learn that in the Hero's Journey, most heroes are reluctant and some may have to be called repeatedly.

Children entering school have no option but to accept this particular call to action. They are, after all, legally required to attend, and the vast majority do so. However, this does not absolve teachers from their responsibility as motivators of learning. Physical attendance may be assured, but the inward quest may be refused with an individual learner drifting off into a life of non-engagement.

Stop and think: Have you responded recently to a 'call to action'?
Can you remember a personal call to action that you accepted? How did it come about? Were you reluctant initially? What made you accept the call?

Comment
The call usually comes when an individual recognises that it is time for a change. The trigger could be a casual remark, a project that requires new thinking and a new approach, or a changed relationship. There is no reason to believe that an externally motivated

---

change, such as transferring from Primary to Secondary education is less potent than a more random one.

One of the many challenges facing teachers is to identify what it is that makes learners want to undertake the quest. In terms of the archetypes (see page 16), at this stage the teacher is acting in the role of herald. The herald brings news, announces a challenge or offers an opportunity. The messenger may mirror the hero in some way, but his main function is to declare that change is on the way. The herald and mentor may be one and the same individual. How can the learning adventure be announced in such a way that learners will respond?

Creating a vision

Organisations around the world have taken up the idea of the inspiring power of a vision. Many have representations of the vision displayed in their offices and printed on their stationery. They have recognised that when individuals feel part of an overall vision they are more purposive, work more efficiently, become absorbed and are prepared to put in extra effort. Among other things, Tom Peters (*Thriving on Chaos*, Pan, 1988) has suggested that a vision should be:

- concise
- clear and challenging
- stable, but constantly challenged
- looking to the future, but honouring the past
- lived in detail, not broad brush strokes.

There are many examples of individuals who have been inspired by their vision.

> As a boy, John always had a poster of the latest and most powerful motor bike on the wall of his bedroom. Nothing unusual in that, but long before he could legally ride such bikes, he knew all about their strengths and weaknesses, and how much they cost.
>
> Helen changed the posters of pop stars on her bedroom wall too. And like John, she used them to create an image of herself as she wanted to be. She didn't just look at the posters and dream; she always asked, *'What is it that makes this one so popular?'*
>
> John went to work selling bikes for a medium-sized dealership, becoming sales manager in his mid-twenties. Helen had a number of hit records before she was sixteen.

These stories clearly represent different kinds of success, but both examples point to the influence that the posters on the wall had on their lives. They were powerful visual representations of what the individuals wanted to achieve. They were aspirations that formed part of an overall vision.

For an individual, the value of a personal vision lies in its power to motivate action and sustain effort. A vision can empower people to do things they never dreamed possible because through the vision they acquire the confidence to try.

Some learners, like John and Helen, will already have an idea of what they want to become when they arrive in Secondary school. They will see themselves as excelling at sport, working with animals or children, and perhaps earning high wages. We know that many of these visions will change, which is just as well since not everyone can be rich and successful in the simplified way that children understand. However, there is nothing wrong with having high aspirations; indeed, many teachers wish that their students' aspirations were higher than they are. Aspirations form a good basis on which to refine a personal vision further.

Most learners will not have started to think in this way. They may never have been inspired to create a personal image or even encouraged to think ahead.

Stop and think: Developing a vision

How do you create a vision that is practical and achievable? Where do you start? The answers to questions like these are not easy, but they are the key to raising the aspirations of learners.

Comment

There is no formula that works for everyone in developing a vision. There are some steps that can be taken, but they are unlikely to succeed in all cases. One of the key factors in leading others to a vision of themselves is commitment on the part of the teacher. Unless you believe that this is an important part of a developmental process and feel fully committed to it, the individuals you are working with will feel that they are engaged in an empty exercise.

Some suggestions that may help learners to refine their vision are suggested under *What can teachers do?*, on page 48–9.

A vision is a glimpse of what the individual can become. It is not a detailed road map, but stands at the top of a hierarchy of other 'guides to action', which the teacher will recognise.

Vision

↑

Aims

↑

Objectives

↑

Targets

↑

Milestones

↑

Individual success is built from the bottom up and the top down. But unless there is clarity about where the aims and objectives are ultimately leading, all the other activities may become haphazard and erratic.

The guidelines set out below are not a once-and-for-all technique; they require review and revision. In developing a vision:

● **explain to learners that they need a vision now**

A vision should be relatively stable, so it should be expected to last for some time, but learners should not spend too much time finalising a precise vision at an early stage in their school careers. They need something that will stimulate thought and aspirations, but is flexible enough to develop over time.

● **encourage learners to draw on their previous experiences**

Learners will arrive in a school or an individual classroom with a previous history. Some of these experiences will be negative and children will need to be encouraged to discount them, but they will also have some positive experiences. What was best about their past? There are numerous inspiring and encouraging examples you can use of people like Winston Churchill who did not do well in school, yet succeeded in life. Equally, there are examples of people who used their formal education as a springboard into subsequent success. Explain to learners that they can leave their past behind. In particular explain to them that temperament is not destiny; that is, they can change and be a different person if they want to be.

- **encourage the development of role models**

  We live at a time when revelations about the private lives of our heroes make the idea of adopting a role model appear naive and childish. Nevertheless, using the successes of others to guide our actions can still be inspiring. Precisely where individuals find role models will be a personal matter. Teachers can perform a valuable service by drawing attention to the features that constitute a role model, and then invite individuals to explore who would be appropriate for them.

- **make it vivid**

  A vision needs to stand out in some way. This could be achieved either by the tightness of the wording, an arresting image or some visual association. For John and Helen in the anecdote recounted earlier (page 45), it was the posters in their bedrooms that made their visions memorable and striking. The vision should shine through all the other images and attitudes that get in the way of an individual achieving his potential.

- **live the vision first**

  In the process of formulating and then living a vision, inconsistencies will inevitably appear. For this reason, it is best if learners find out for themselves whether their vision accurately reflects their aspirations. It is also important for the teacher to have a vision and communicate it to learners. The vision need not reveal anything personal, but could refer entirely to learner success.

- **encourage wide thinking but tight wording**

  A vision needs to be closely woven, but inform all areas of life. For example, the vision could refer to intellectual life, skills, work, social standing, appearance and wealth.

WHAT CAN TEACHERS DO?

1 Encourage active thinking about a personal vision, with doodling, lists and provisional sketches.

2 Set objectives for every lesson, which are explicitly communicated to learners. Review whether the objectives have been achieved at the end of the lesson. Demonstrate how those objectives support your vision of yourself as a teacher of a classroom full of successful learners.

3 If children have negative experiences of learning, encourage them to think '*I used to be like that, but not any longer.*' How can this attitude be projected forward into their future?

4 In drawing up a vision, ask learners to consider:

   - intellectual achievements (What kind of knowledge will they have?)

   - skill levels (What skills will they have acquired?)

   - work (What kind of a job will they have? At what level will they be working?)

- social standing (How will they be perceived by others?)

- money (How much money will they be earning?)

- physical appearance (What will they look like? How fit will they be?).

5 Remember that constructing a vision is a very personal activity and it is futile to pretend that there is only one way of going about it. For example, you could ask learners to 'review' their vision by suggesting that they should write their own obituary, possibly after studying those of others in the newspapers first.

Barriers to forming a vision

Some people prefer not to be inspired or to take up the challenge of creating a vision because the prospect of personal development and change makes them feel uncomfortable. Most children in school will at least comply when a teacher asks them to develop a personal vision, but resistance may take many forms. Some individuals may:

- **see themselves as too 'down-to-earth'**

  People like this may see themselves as having a very practical turn of mind. They may argue that worrying about anything as abstract as a personal vision is futile. In terms of preferred learning strategies, this kind of person may well be a pragmatist.

- **not have the time to reflect on such ideas**

  Many people are easily distracted. Some – for example, those who show a preference for an activist learning strategy – will seek out novelty and prefer the drama of risk-taking. None of these characteristics deny the possibility of forming a sustaining vision, but they do tend to diminish the likelihood of the necessary reflection and personal analysis taking place. Do not be surprised if these people throw themselves into the 'visioning' exercises at first, but be prepared for them to lose interest rapidly.

- **not feel worthy**

  It is comfortable to stay in a known and understood world rather than launch into something new and demanding. For those people who are too attached to their comfort zone, it is easier to remain shielded by a self-perception of being 'just an ordinary person', of whom little is demanded or expected, than to strive for success.

- **feel they know all the answers**

  Again, this may be a defensive response. The individual does not want the challenge of something new and may refuse to take the activity seriously.

All of the above types need to undergo a process of change in order to develop a personal vision.

WHAT CAN TEACHERS DO?

1   Explain to the group that they are going to embark on a series of exercises, which may be very personal. Go on to say that they only need to share those feelings about which they are confident. Aim for them to have a vision statement fairly quickly, but make sure that everyone understands that it will only be provisional.

2   Encourage learners to find out about successful people and how they remain positive and at the very top of their profession. Tell your own stories to amplify the idea of a sustaining vision (for example, Anita Roddick and The Body Shop; Richard Branson and Virgin – although the subjects do not have to be famous for the stories to be effective).

3   While some people are happy to write down their ideas, others prefer to think in visual terms; that is, they prefer to draw pictures. Invite learners to devise a 'coat of arms' for themselves based on their personal vision. This is usually represented as a shield, but you could use other forms if you prefer. Use each section of the shield to represent different parts of the personality. For example you could designate quarters for social, professional, domestic and sporting life.

4   Suggest devising a logo to encapsulate the vision. Use well-known examples to explain how a logo is specifically devised to have an immediate impact and to be easily recognised.

5   Ask learners to find out the motto of any organisation or group that they admire. One professional football team has the motto *Arte et Labore* ('skill and diligence'). Point out that mottos represent vision statements, but also add that they do not necessarily have to be in Latin!

6   Ask members of the group how they would change their behaviour if their chosen role model were standing at their shoulder, watching over them every minute of the day.

Programme of action

Defining a vision is a first step. How can it be converted into a series of day-to-day activities that build to success?

Once a personal vision begins to form, the next stage is to clarify how it can be translated into a programme of action. This means defining some aims and objectives. These represent the short-term steps that an individual can take to achieve her goals.

The material that follows may be used directly with learners, although it may need to be introduced gradually. It is intended to be used as part of the 'toolkit' that learners take with them on their journey.

Aims and objectives

Aims may be defined as guidelines for action. They indicate the general direction in which an individual should go. An **objective**, on the other hand, is a specific goal to be achieved while travelling in a known direction. Aims may be expressed in the very broadest terms while objectives should be about the steps to be taken on the way to achieving the aims.

Objectives:

- describe the final result of an action
- are specific and precise
- describe a change that can be measured or observed
- specify an endpoint for an activity.

Objectives should begin by using verbs such as:

- construct
- clarify
- define
- determine
- establish

- evaluate
- explain
- identify
- learn
- review.

If you intend to encourage learners to use objectives for themselves, they will need some training in how to write them: it does not come naturally. One way of demonstrating the value of objectives is to set aside a few minutes at the beginning of every lesson to state explicitly what the learning objectives are and what should be achieved by the end. Not only does this offer an opportunity to demonstrate how objectives should be written, it also establishes the teacher's own commitment.

The more unequivocal individuals can be about what they want to achieve, the more likely they are to reach their goals.

> **Stop and think: How often do you use objectives?**
> What were your objectives for the last session you taught? Did they conform with the 'rules' set out above?

Targets

Once you have clarified your aims and objectives, the next stage is to define the **targets** and **milestones**. Continuing the metaphor of the journey, the targets are indications that you are on the right track and milestones tell you how far you have come.

You may have encountered the idea of SMART targets before. This is a useful acronym that helps to keep your activities focused. SMART targets are:

Specific	they go into enough detail
Measurable	you know when you have reached them
Achievable	the targets may be demanding, but they can be reached
Realistic	the work can be done within the resources available
Timebound	time limits are set.

Stop and think: Can you apply the concept of SMART targets to your teaching?
Select a number of targets drawn from your professional life. Analyse their 'SMARTness' using a grid similar to the one set out in Table 3.1.

Alternatively, if you are not used to using SMART targets, you could apply the technique to a personal project just to see how it works. For example, you could use SMART targets when changing your car or planning a holiday.

Table 3.1 Grid for analysing how SMART your targets are

Objective: display work more effectively	Target A: All students to have work on the walls twice in a year	Target B: Work to be used as an active part of lessons	...
Specific?			
Measurable?			
Achievable?			
Realistic?			
Timebound?			

Milestones

When you have your aims, objectives and targets, then the final step is to set the milestones for achievement.

Useful as targets are, on their own they are not enough. No matter how SMART, they will require careful control as they are implemented. Therefore, when you are planning you should build in intermediate stages or milestones in order to monitor progress. Milestones are indicators of progress, which have to be reached by a certain time in order to guarantee completion of the overall task. One commonly used technique for scheduling milestones is the Gantt chart.

The Gantt chart is a graph that shows all the activities to be undertaken in a project on the vertical scale and the time available on the horizontal. Black lines running across the chart show how long each activity should last. The chart can be refined by using black lines for essential activities and grey (or any other colour) lines for desirable ones. The advantage of this technique is that it sets out the stages of work to be done in a clear, visual form. A simplified example is given opposite.

Activities	Sept	Oct	Nov	Dec	Jan	Feb
Introduce	▬▬					
Develop		▬▬▬▬▬▬				
Test					▬	
Revise					▬	
Evaluate						▬▬

Gantt charts are very useful for giving a visual representation of the staging of work throughout the year. However, you should remember to build in to your scheduling slippage time for foreseeable delays such as holidays and unforeseeable ones such as illness.

Stop and think: How can you make use of Gantt charts?
Gantt charts can be used either as a personal planning tool or as a wall display demonstrating progress towards an agreed goal for the whole class.

● Where could you use one to keep a visual record of progress towards agreed aims?

● Could you use Gantt charts as a tool for planning and implementing a revision programme?

WHAT CAN TEACHERS DO?

1 Introduce your objectives by writing on the board 'By the end of this lesson you will be able to ...'

2 Limit the number of objectives to between three and five for each lesson.

3 Try to set aside a space on the board so that the objectives remain on view throughout the lesson and do not get cleared off to accommodate other work.

4 At the end of a lesson, discuss possible objectives for the next lesson. Involving learners in setting lesson objectives promotes a sense of ownership.

5 To practise using Gantt charts, simply choose any activity, whether personal or professional, and use a chart to plan how the activity will develop over time.

SUMMARY

◆ THERE ARE A NUMBER OF PRACTICAL STEPS THAT CAN BE TAKEN TO FORMULATE A PERSONAL VISION.

◆ LEARNERS NEED EXPLICIT INSTRUCTION IN HOW TO WRITE OBJECTIVES.

◆ TEACHERS CAN DEMONSTRATE THE PRACTICAL VALUE OF A PERSONAL VISION AND SHORT-TERM OBJECTIVES BY MAKING EXPLICIT REFERENCE TO THEM IN LESSONS.

Meeting the mentor

In Section Four we learn that:

- Mentoring is a key activity for teachers.

- There are a number of differing forms for conducting one-to-one discussions.

- Appropriate questioning techniques and active listening are essential for successful mentoring.

BACKGROUND

The meeting with the mentor represents a turning point for the hero. It is through the mentor that heroes begin to gather the necessary resources of determination and confidence, and supplies of skill and knowledge, that they will need for the journey.

A successful relationship with a mentor is the key to success in undertaking the Hero's Journey. In *The Wizard of Oz*, Dorothy encounters many mentors such as Professor Marvel and Glinda, the Good Witch. Heroes may also encounter negative forces that appear to be mentors. For example, the witches in *Macbeth* act as mentors, but their effect is evil – in fact, the witches are archetypally closer to shadows or tricksters. Mentors are usually human, but they could also take the form of an animal, a set of rules, a moral code or some other reference point for guiding action. In ancient myth it may be one of the gods who guides the hero, and even in more contemporary stories the mentor may appear to have superhuman powers of insight and understanding.

Emotion is a vital element in the relationship. How the hero and mentor feel about each other is just as important as any technical knowledge that the mentor may impart to the hero. Frequently, a mentor will take on the role of parent. However, the mentor must guard against being over-protective. Her job is to guide action and set the individual on the path, not undertake the journey on the hero's behalf.

The mentor's role is a temporary one, since the hero must transcend the need for a mentor as the journey progresses. This inevitably happens in schools where children have set leaving dates, after which most learners lose contact with their teacher. Some hero–mentor relationships continue, but not in their original form.

The mentor maps out the road ahead, and will probably have undertaken a similar quest to the one the hero is about to begin. She may be able to help the hero forward when he gets stuck, but there her power ends. The role of the mentor is to:

- protect
- guide
- teach
- test
- train
- provide gifts that will support the individual in his quest.

Learners can expect to have a number of mentors throughout their lifetimes. This is because we all undertake a succession of journeys and learn different lessons from each.

Stop and think: Who are (or were) your mentors?

- Who are the people who have acted as mentors for you? How did they influence you?

- Was each mentor a person or did something else – for example, an object or an idea – act in the role?

- How do you use the influence of your past mentors now? Do they still guide your actions in some way?

APPLICATION

Consider this brief account of a first day at school.

> I'd heard all sorts of stories about the Secondary school. I was thinking about it all summer holidays. I got a really bad attack of nerves when I got up for the first morning. The school was not far from where I lived, so I had no trouble getting there, but then I had to walk past all the older kids who were coming back. It felt like everyone was looking at me.
>
> It didn't feel so bad when I spotted some of my mates from Junior school, and of course, whatever happened we couldn't show we were scared. The next thing I knew we were lining up in the playground and one of the teachers was

reading out names. I didn't understand what was going on because I already knew what class I was in, even how to find the classroom because we had visited the school last term. Suddenly this big kid was standing in front of me and said, 'Come on, Warren, you're with me.' I wasn't sure why, but I followed him. He took me to my first class and told me he'd be waiting when I got out.

He kept asking me questions like, 'Going OK?' and I always said 'Yeah'. Couldn't think of anything else to say, but you could tell nobody messed with him. He made sure that nobody messed with me. He was the one who told me to go to the toilet before I left home so I didn't have to go in school and showed me how to stay out of the way of some kids who were trouble.

After a couple of days, I didn't need him any more. I'd never said I needed him in the first place, even when I did, but inside I was glad he was there. After that, when I saw him in the corridor, we would just look at each other, sometimes he would wink.

Stop and think: How does your school use mentors?
- Does your school have a scheme where younger students are mentored, as in the extract above? What are the advantages and disadvantages?

- Do you think a scheme that sets up mentors explicitly will work, or do individuals have to find their own mentors without 'official' interference?

The personal qualities of the mentor

A mentor always represents a positive force. Mentors may see their role as being one that provokes fresh thinking and stimulates action, but this is never a destructive impulse. Alternatively, the mentor may be seen as the better part of ourselves, perhaps acting as a conscience helping us to distinguish right or wrong. This kind of 'internal' mentor may only develop after the learner has experienced the direct influence of an 'external' mentor.

The teacher, acting in the demanding role of mentor, should select an approach that suits the specific needs of the individual. Some schools use older students in a mentoring capacity, but many experts believe that mentoring is too onerous for the relatively inexperienced and should only be carried out by someone older and more seasoned.

Stop and think: What are the personal qualities needed by a mentor?
Clarify for yourself at least five characteristics of the ideal mentor.

Comment
You may have written down a list of qualities something like the one below.

A mentor must be:
- *a positive role model*
- *sufficiently experienced and qualified to be credible in offering guidance*
- *sympathetic to the difficulties of the learner*
- *a good listener*
- *a good motivator*
- *discreet, within the limits of the best interests of the individual and the organisation*
- *capable of viewing the role of mentor as a development opportunity for himself as well as for the individual.*

The mentor should enable the learner to function independently as soon as possible, though this does not mean that their relationship will simply end. The individual teacher may continue to support a learner once he has left his class.

The key activities for a mentor are to:

- help to maximise the opportunities for learning

- recognise turning points in the learner's development and offer appropriate guidance

- guide the individual into harmonious relationships.

A mentor need not necessarily be someone with a lot of patience. Many excellent mentors are demanding, setting high standards and exacting goals. However, successful mentors of this type are also realistic about an individual's abilities and put extra effort into ensuring that their high expectations can be met. Mentors of this type must also be very high on credibility: they should be able to demonstrate that they are expert in whatever they are demanding from the learner.

Stop and think: How good a mentor are you?
Now that you have thought about the personal qualities needed by a mentor, use the questions set out below to review where you might need training or development. This activity requires honest appraisal, not false modesty!

- Why is mentoring important?
- What are the skills needed by a mentor that you already possess?
- Where do you need development? What can you do about developing the skills you need?
- Are different kinds of mentoring skills required in different situations?

Comment

The aim of mentoring is to help the individual through difficult periods of rapid growth and change. A mentor does this by interpreting and explaining aspects of the learner's situation to him, or helping him to adjust to change. To demonstrate that he has understood the lessons the mentor has to teach, the learner should internalise a set of rules, learn new skills or absorb important information.

The mentor sets a series of challenges for the learner, but should not undertake any part of the journey on his behalf. The key element in hero–mentor relationships is that heroes must undertake the journey themselves; mentors can only advise. This may lead to false starts, mistakes and disappointments, but for the mentor to undertake too much responsibility would be a betrayal of the essence of the relationship.

Experience has shown that mentors, whether officially appointed or 'found' by the hero, make a difference. They can:

- help learners to 'fit in' more rapidly

- improve commitment

- clarify the new roles for learners at every stage of their school careers.

In addition, those who act in the role of mentor experience considerable job satisfaction. The most intensive period of mentoring occurs at the beginning of the journey. For example, a school may have an induction period, which (unconsciously) asks the learner to 'cross the threshold' as well as 'meet the mentor'. Normally, induction lasts for a fixed period of time and may have practical as well as emotional objectives. The school may, for instance, want to ensure that new learners are integrated gradually by bringing them in a day earlier than the rest of the school, temporarily sectioning off parts for their exclusive use and providing guides to help them transfer from one lesson to another.

WHAT CAN TEACHERS DO?

If your school has an induction period for younger learners where older students act as mentors, or is planning to implement one, you may want to consider the following points.

1 Before the first meeting, identify the type of mentoring needed. Make sure that individuals who have been asked to act as mentors understand their role. Naturally, you will select only those older students that you think can do the job, but even the level-headed types will require guidance. Tell them that they should clarify their relationship with the younger learner at the first meeting. Right from the start all parties need to understand the rules and procedures they should follow. These rules may cover:

- what the mentor will do to help the younger learner

- when meetings will take place (perhaps mentors will collect younger learners from one class and take them on to the next)

- any other times they will meet.

2 Explain to mentors that, in the beginning, they should take the lead but as the relationship develops, and the younger learners develop a sense of their own independence, they should hand over control.

3 At the end of the induction period the mentor should devise some way of bringing the process to an unequivocal conclusion. This does not mean that the need for a mentor is at an end – only that the close of the mentor/induction process should be marked. This may involve something like a letter of congratulation from the headteacher.

Naturally, teachers will be acting in mentoring roles throughout the induction period as well.

Stop and think: What do learners require from a mentor at different stages?
How would you characterise the different needs of the three types of learner given below?
- the year 7 student just beginning in your school
- a older learner you have never met before and who is just starting in one of your classes
- the older learner with whom you are familiar, perhaps just beginning a new term or unit of work

Comment
Among other things, you probably identified the Y7 learner as being in need of:
- *general information about you and your subject*
- *reassurance, particularly on the first day*
- *specific needs relevant to your subject (for example, workshop/laboratory safety).*

The older student that you are meeting for the first time may have fewer immediate needs, but she will certainly require:
- *reassurance about how you value her as an individual*
- *guidance on communications and personal and social relationships within your classroom*
- *an introduction to others in the group if they have not worked together before.*

Finally, the learner with whom you are familiar may need:
- *reassurance about your relationship (how will it have changed and developed from previous involvement – perhaps you can treat him more as an adult now?)*
- *information about the new work he will be doing and the standards he is expected to achieve*
- *how you expect him to take on greater individual responsibility.*

Mentoring in one-to-one discussions

At the end of induction, both the individual learner and the mentor instinctively know that their relationship will change. The next stage is to develop the relationship. The most powerful context for doing this is the one-to-one discussion.

The teacher may use a one-to-one discussion to engage in any one of a range of activities, depending on the individual involved. However, in every case, there is an emphasis on the role of language as a key activity, which will have repercussions on the outcome. The focus here is on teachers interacting with learners, but inferences may be drawn about discussions with colleagues and parents as well.

Language is important to teachers, no matter what the context. It is particularly important in a one-to-one situation because of the imbalance of power between the teacher and the learner and the potential this has for generating misunderstanding. Competency in handling interviews of this kind cannot be achieved by following a set of rules or tactics, but rather it comes about when teachers are sensitive to the effects language can have and develop personal skills that can be adapted to the needs of a particular situation.

Stop and think: What are the contexts for mentoring?
Most learners see their teacher in a whole-class teaching context. However, most effective mentoring happens one-to-one. Other than the times when you engineer a one-to-one discussion, when do such interactions 'naturally' occur? For example, detaining someone who has not done their homework, after a lesson, might be one such opportunity.

Comment
A teacher may find opportunities for mentoring when she:
- *discusses a year-end report*
- *reprimands an unruly student after a lesson*
- *discusses an essay with a sixth-former*
- *interviews an individual to find out who was responsible for an anti-social act*
- *advises a learner just before an examination.*

In some subjects, such as technology and PE, individual coaching and one-to-one discussion is more common. If you find that there is little use made of this powerful teaching mechanism in your subject, or it is only used in a disciplinary context, perhaps you might like to consider ways in which it could be deployed more widely.

Once you have reflected on the contexts for mentoring, the next step is to consider the effect a teacher hopes to have in conducting a one-to-one interview. In other words, change the emphasis from the *subject* of the interaction ('year-end report', 'unruly student', 'examination') to its *aim* ('discuss', 'reprimand', 'advise').

Set out overleaf are ten typical situations that teachers encounter when talking to learners on a one-to-one basis. The list is not comprehensive, missing out as it does such typical negotiating situations as 'apologising', 'dismissing' or 'promising'. The ten selected are those most likely to be encountered by classroom teachers. As you read through them, remember that any one situation may require the deployment of a combination of actions to achieve the desired outcome. The actions are:

1   advising

2   asking

3   confirming

4   directing

5   discussing

6   informing

7   negotiating

8   praising

9   reporting

10 reprimanding.

Remember also that while these are not all direct teaching situations (for example, 'reprimanding'), the intention is that learning should nevertheless take place. For each interaction, there is a 'keynote', which offers a central issue to be considered when communicating with a learner; some comments on the context for learning and some sentence forms, which may help you to identify typical situations in which such an interaction might happen.

1   Advising

Keynote
The teacher expects to have influence over learners, but not to coerce them.

The emphasis here is on recommending a particular course of action. Care should be exercised to ensure that the learner sees the recommended actions as lying within the domain of the teacher. If not, there will be resistance. Teachers may take considerable liberties with offering advice because they are recognised as possessing authority, experience and knowledge. However, forms such as *'You ought to ...'* may be resented since they seem to take final control of the learner's actions away from the individual.

Forms
- *'If I were you, I would ...'*
- *'I suggest ...'*
- *'Why don't you ask ... about that?'*
- *'In this situation most people would ...'*

2   Asking

Keynote
The teacher seeks to produce new information or clarify given data.

An understanding of the use of open and closed questions is important in this context, but rhetorical questions also assume greater significance in one-to-one discussions because of their power to express strong feelings: *'Didn't I tell you that would happen?'*; *'For heaven's sake, what difference does it make?'* Asking is different from 'questioning' or 'querying' since it does not imply disagreement about a point. Teachers should be careful about using what linguists call 'illocutionary force' in an utterance; that is, disguising an instruction as an indirect question: *'Can we talk about your problem now?'* Such subtleties are not always understood by learners, who may well answer, *'No'*.

Forms
(Please see *Asking the right questions*, page 67.)

3 Confirming

Keynote
The teacher adds his own weight to a thought or idea that has been expressed earlier.

Confirming can be a powerful act, verifying the link between the teacher and the student. It may be partial or total in its application; that is, there may be complete or limited agreement with a previously stated idea or point of view.

Forms

- *'I want to confirm what we talked about last week.'* (total)

- *'That is reasonable, but there is one small point I want to add ...'* (partial)

- *'I agree with you on one point, but there is a lot we need to discuss.'* (limited)

4 Directing

Keynote
The teacher acts as an authority, in the way that a film director guides an actor, but is not necessarily ordering a course of action.

The teacher assumes that the student will comply, but prefers a rational justification that allows the individual room for personal interpretation. This is not just a face-saving exercise, but a genuine engagement that opens the possibility of an alternative reading of a situation. Teachers often use this form when they do not want to appear to be too aggressive. However, directing also relies to some extent on illocutionary force and may not be clear enough for some learners. 'Ordering' is much stronger and may be a next step if the teacher encounters resistance.

Forms

- *'When can I see your work? I think you should get it done as soon as possible because ...'*

- *'It's probably time to think about doing ..., don't you agree?'*

5 Discussing

Keynote
Teacher and learner are placed on an equal footing and engage in genuine consultation. Both parties are unsure of what they think about a topic, where it might lead and what the outcome might be.

Discussion lies between 'talking something over' (since it suggests a clearer purpose to the activity) and 'debate' (which is much more formal, implying rules of interaction and the possibility of winners and losers). Both partners need to show trust in discussion. However, because of the unequal nature of the teacher–learner relationship, it is usually up to the teacher to win the confidence of the student and draw her into discussion. Unfortunately, the learner often perceives an expression of opinion in the teacher's invitation to enter into discussion. Students may need to be convinced of the sincerity of your enquiry.

Forms

- *'I'd like to know what you think about ...'*
- *'I think you are not working as hard as you should. What about you?'* (expression of opinion or invitation to discuss?)
- *'Can we think a little more about this?'* ('we' or 'you'?)

6 Informing

Keynote
Teachers act in the traditional role of imparting knowledge to others.

The situation in which a one-to-one session is used to impart knowledge is relatively rare, though not unknown, in schools. It is more common in further and higher education. If it is to be used with younger learners, the expectations of the teacher may need to be set out at the beginning of the session. For example, it might be helpful to clarify how long the session will last; what is going to happen (that is, what phases the session will have); what the agenda is and whether notes should be taken.

Forms

- *'I want to talk about ...'*
- *'It is essential that you understand ...'*

7 Negotiating

Keynote
The teacher and the learner need to agree on something (usually a course of action) before progress can be made.

Teachers use negotiating skills more often than you might expect. This is because most want to carry learners along with them rather than put them in a position of having to comply with an order. Consequently, a teacher might extend a deadline for an essay or agree to a certain kind of seating arrangement in the classroom. Negotiating like this can appear inconsistent to some students who do not benefit from the terms of the agreement. For this reason and others, teachers are rightly wary of allowing too many concessions and should always rigorously enforce the other half of the settlement ('*If I agree to ... then you must do ...*'). For this reason, the best context for negotiation is the one-to-one session.

Forms

- '*What we must aim at is ...*'

- '*Do you agree that this is what needs to be done?*'

- '*These are our possible options ... Which do you think is the right one for you?*'

- '*Let's check to be sure that we have agreed what we are going to do. I am going to ... while you are going to ...*'

8 Praising

Keynote
Teachers use good performance to stimulate learners to further development.

To be really effective, praise should be specific. '*Your work is improving*' may lead to a warm glow for learners, but it does not help them to build on good performance. '*You were much more detailed in your account of the experiment and you remembered to label your diagrams this time*', will also encourage the learner, but the details of how improvement was achieved will help to develop skills and understanding further. However, it is worth occasionally offering praise for its own sake without always adding a 'next step', which somehow seems to imply that the last one was not good enough. For some students, 'praising' may need the same kind of privacy as 'reprimanding'.

Forms

- '*Well done. That was good because ...*'

- '*What I particularly liked about your work was ...*'

9 Reporting

Keynote
Teachers are expected to fulfil the role of reporter in the sense that they assess performance and provide feedback to the learner on progress.

The written report, coming at the end of an academic year, is very often criticised for being vague. The reasons for this are complex, but a central concern is the immutable nature of writing – you have to be very careful about what you put on paper because it is always there to be used as evidence. The one-to-one session offers a much more intimate opportunity to go into detail about performance.

Forms

- '*Your last piece of work lacked detail. Look at this ...*'

- '*I want to talk to you about ...*'

10 Reprimanding

Keynote

The teacher communicates a negative judgement about a learner's performance.

Whether the individual is an adult or the youngest learner, reprimands are best administered in a one-to one session. This is because the potential for humiliation is so great. The intention of a reprimand should be to improve performance, and therefore a reprimand can be a teaching act. Any sense of injustice felt by the subject of a rebuke will militate against her learning from it. Therefore the person administering the reprimand should possess the necessary authority, should not be guilty of the same or similar faults (*'It's all very well you telling me off for not doing my homework – but you haven't marked our books this term!'*) and should establish the facts unequivocally at the beginning. One of the greatest mistakes made by those issuing a reprimand is to deny the individual the space to maintain his self-respect. Make sure that there is an escape route for the individual; for example, a sincere apology, a promise to do better in the future or, best of all, an unequivocal promise to make up any deficiencies.

Forms

- *'Is it true that ...'* (establish the facts)

- *'This is the way I see it.'*

- *'What you have done is not acceptable; in future you must ...'*

Remember that a single one-to-one session may involve a number of these forms. A 'reprimand' may develop into a 'negotiation'. The key point for the teacher is to know in advance which forms will be required and then plan for their deployment.

> **WHAT CAN TEACHERS DO?**
>
> 1 Briefly, clarify what you want to get out of an interview or discussion before you start. (If you have made a note of the time of a meeting in your diary, add two or three negotiating forms as well by way of preparation.)
>
> 2 If there is no formal agenda for the discussion, set out some ideas for yourself.
>
> 3 Have some key words in your head that will take the discussion forward.
>
> 4 Make brief notes to evaluate whether the discussion went as you expected. (This is useful for your learning as well as providing a simple record of what happened.)

Stop and think: What can you learn from your own experience of interviews?

Think back over any of the interviews or one-to-one discussions you have attended where you felt ill at ease for reasons well beyond the natural nervousness everyone experiences on such occasions. What was the reason for your discomfort?

Comment

Generally, people experience discomfort during interviews or discussions because of their own fear of failure, but there may also be a lack of preparation or rude and thoughtless behaviour on the part of the interviewer. You may be able to recall occasions when:

- *'He was sitting behind this big desk.'*
- *'The sun was directly in my face.'*
- *'I could not see her eyes with the lights glinting off her glasses.'*
- *'I felt so inferior with him sitting up high and me on this low chair.'*
- *'The telephone kept ringing – at one point she left the room altogether to deal with some crisis.'*

In other words, we can be put off by the physical setting of an interview as much as by the thoughtlessness of the interviewer. Teachers are not always in a position to organise the setting for a one-to-one session in advance since most will be unplanned and take place in a classroom or in the corridor, but where it is feasible you might pay attention to:

- *creating an informal setting*
- *finding neutral ground*
- *providing comfortable chairs*
- *ensuring that no-one is seated behind a desk*
- *possibly having coffee or tea available*
- *making sure there are no telephones or other interruptions.*

These factors may not be appropriate to some situations, of course, such as 'reprimanding'.

Asking the right questions

Open and closed questions are a key part of the success of one-to-one teaching. **Open questions** can be used to:

- clarify ideas and hopes

- provoke thinking

- develop positive mental attitudes

- 'open up' an individual so that she talks more freely than she might in a group setting

- make an individual feel as if he is involved in a discussion, and not being interrogated.

Closed questions are used to:

- clarify facts
- extract detailed information
- identify a personal position ('yes/no' questions)
- close down a discussion and move on.

Most one-to-one teaching situations will move from closed questions to open questions. This is because the first step should always be to establish common ground by asking factual questions where you can find agreement, then move to more open-ended questions that invite reflection and, possibly, areas of disagreement. Starting with closed questions also helps to build trust since you begin from where the individual feels strongest – talking about themselves.

Typical examples of closed questions might include:

- *'Which books did you use to help with this essay?'*
- *'When were you absent from school?'*
- *'Have you completed all the revision for the examination?'*
- *'Is it true that you have not completed any homework for the last month?'*

Open questions might include:

- *'How are you getting on with using the Internet?'*
- *'What do you think are the advantages?'*
- *'How do you think you could use it in your work?'*
- *'What do you want to achieve in the coming year?'*

Seek clarity by using closed questions: seek agreement and adherence to school values through open questions. When you are using one-to-one interactions to discipline a student, begin with closed questions to establish the facts.

Active listening

Just because we hear, it does not mean that we listen.

In fact, our brains are programmed to filter out a considerable amount of the noise that is around us. This is because there is so much to hear, but so little to which we must listen. We pick up the sound, but we do not bother to process it.

WHAT CAN TEACHERS DO?

If you watch experienced interviewers at work, you will probably notice that they have mastered the conventions of 'turn-taking' in conversation. Your students may need coaching in some of these techniques of discussion.

1   The person speaking looks away from the listener, occasionally glancing back to check that attention has been retained, until she is finishing what she has to say, at which point she moves her eyes back to the face of the listener.

2   The listener watches the face of the speaker. (Not to do this is interpreted as a lack of interest.)

3   People will often mirror each other's sitting position; for example, both people in an interview situation might sit cross-legged or with hands folded. (You can use this technique to establish contact with others, but beware of making it too obvious.)

4   The interviewer, if he is being sympathetic, will often make approving noises, say 'yes' and nodding his head to show that he is being attentive. (Beware, however – too much of this can be irritating.)

5   When seeking clarity, the interviewer will often re-phrase what the speaker has said, putting it in a different way. (But be careful not to manipulate the speaker by misrepresenting her.)

6   The interviewer asks questions that call for further thought on an issue. Questions such as *'Why do you think that was?'*, and *'Would you do it differently next time?'*, not only ask for further thought but demonstrate that the interviewer has been listening.

This list gives quite a lot to remember, but if you break it down into stages, it does not seem like so much, and you will be surprised how soon you begin to apply the techniques unconsciously.

Structuring the discussion

It helps to think of the one-to-one discussion as falling into the three broad phases of 'introduction', 'development' and 'conclusion' (Table 4.1).

Structuring the discussion in this way may appear rather formal, but it is only a framework and the learner need not be aware of it. Some might say it is an over-simplification of the process. However, it does offer you some *'Where next?'* signposts and it can help to avoid running over time if you have a deadline.

An additional benefit of structuring the discussion in this way is that at each stage, the teacher can check that appropriate feedback has been given and received.

Table 4.1 Structure of a one-to-one discussion

	Activities at each stage could include:	'Turning points' or key words at each stage might include:
Introduction	breaking the ice setting the agenda declaring the teacher's role (advisor, organiser, regulator) reviewing previous discussions	*'Yes, I agree with your **summary** of our last meeting.'* *'You have **achieved** a lot since we last spoke.'* *'**Practising** really seems to have helped; what is the next step?'*
Development	asking for opinions discussing improvements offering assistance to improve performance discussing possible targets	*'Can we build on this **achievement**?'* *'You reached that **target** with ease – should it have been more ambitious?'* *'I like the way you **developed** ...'*
Conclusion	setting new targets calling for final thoughts summarising the discussion agreeing action	*'Let me **check** that I have got this straight.'* *'Would it **help** if ...'* *'I think we have **covered** all the things we wanted to discuss. Is there anything you want to add?'*

Constructive criticism

Sometimes you have to tell learners that they are not doing well. What do you do? The rules are simple enough to put on a page, but far more difficult to apply in practice. Begin by establishing the facts:

- *'Is it true that … ?'*

Try to avoid making accusations. Very often, the person concerned knows that things are not right and will volunteer information. Probe a little further:

- *'Are you aware of the problem?'*
- *'Why is it happening?'*
- *'Are personal circumstances affecting your work?'* (Be understanding, but make it clear that poor performance cannot be tolerated.)

Make an honest assessment using the facts:

- *'You were getting B+ for your work last term. Recently you seem to be getting all Cs or less. Can we get back to at least a B?'*

Offer support and emphasise the positive where you can:

- *'Would it help to work in the library at lunch time?'*
- *'Should I change where you sit in class?'*
- *'I think you would benefit if I talked to your parents about this.'*

WHAT CAN TEACHERS DO?

1   When planning an interview like this you must:

- check the facts before you begin – don't rely solely on the opinions of others – and check them again with the individual: *'Is it true that … ?'*

- get the individual to tell you what is going wrong, if possible (but avoid, *'Why do you think you are here?'*)

- be sure that if you are going to offer something during the interview that you have the authority to do so.

2   When giving negative feedback, sandwich the bad bits between the good. In the three-phase structure (introduction–development–conclusion), give something positive at the beginning, put the negatives in the middle and return to the positive at the end. Trust is crucial and learners are prepared to accept the negative if it is given in a way that acknowledges the positive.

3   Agree an action plan for improvement. The plan should be reviewed, formally or informally, within a month to six weeks.

A final word

One of the characteristics of the mentor in many myths and stories is that he often gives some kind of gift to the hero. This may be a tool, a weapon or a good luck charm. As a teacher you can give out books, marks and praise. Are there any other 'gifts', apart from these conventional ones, that you can give to your learners?

SUMMARY

- SUCCESSFUL MENTORS SET THE HERO FREE; THEY DO NOT UNDERTAKE THE JOURNEY ON THE HERO'S BEHALF.

- TEACHERS SHOULD GIVE CAREFUL THOUGHT TO THE FORMS OF THE ONE-TO-ONE DISCUSSIONS THEY ARE LIKELY OT ENCOUNTER WITH LEARNERS.

- TO BE EFFECTIVE, PRAISE NEEDS TO BE DETAILED AND IMMEDIATE.

Crossing the threshold

In Section Five we learn that:

- Crossing the threshold is a key stage in learning.

- An understanding of change management can help teachers to guide learners through this stage.

BACKGROUND

The hero takes up the challenge of the journey. The first threshold may herald a series of others, but the initial decision represents a watershed for the hero.

The motivation may come from the desire either to leave behind an unhappy situation or to move towards something better. These may in fact be 'push' and 'pull' factors – merely different sides of the same coin. For example, in *Star Wars*, Luke Skywalker is unhappy with the humdrum domesticity of his life on the farm long before the Imperial Storm Troopers kill his uncle and aunt. It is this decisive moment of violence that hurls him into the adventure. However, in *Othello* the motivation is very different. Beguiled by his evil shadow Iago, Othello crosses the threshold into jealousy when he sees his wife speaking to Cassio.

One of the characteristics of the hero's new world is that the old rules no longer apply. The noble, but naive, Othello is at a loss in the shadowy world of intrigue and double meaning. The comfortable reference points of the ordinary world no longer apply. Not only must the hero deal with the enemies and allies encountered along the way, but also with the hazards of the road itself. Each step of the journey involves risk, but it is particularly acute at this point.

The problem for the teacher is how to reconcile the excitement of risk-taking with the sense of security that is essential for the growth and development of young learners.

APPLICATION

The techniques of using 'pre-exposure' and 'inception' activities with learners are explored in Section Twelve under the heading of *Learning design* (see page 169). That first impression is vital with learners and it is worth devoting considerable creative energy to getting it right. However, since crossing the threshold entails understanding and managing change, the remainder of this Section is concerned with providing teachers with an overall understanding of the processes involved.

This Section sets out a systematic approach to understanding and implementing the management of change. While some of the material is drawn from sources outside education, its application to teaching is clear. The emphasis is on the individual and how approaches to teaching impact on learning. It makes the assumption that individuals are purposeful and will act in their own best interests, but that everyone likes to remain within their own 'comfort zone' of activity. If these personal 'pull' factors imply a little too much optimism, there is a balancing acceptance that 'push' factors, in the form of teacher intervention, will also be needed. In other words, the process of managing change is not a straightforward one and the use of carrots *and* sticks may be necessary.

The starting point is MacGregor's well-known division of managers into Theory 'X' and 'Y', and its implications for teachers. The theory was originally applied to managers in industry, but the broad categories that MacGregor proposes are appropriate for teachers and managers in schools as well.

MacGregor's Theory X and Theory Y

Douglas MacGregor suggested that there are basically two assumptions made by managers about people at work (*The Human Side of Enterprise*, McGraw-Hill, 1960). He characterised these as 'Theory X' and 'Theory Y'. Although MacGregor's work is now over 40 years old, it still provides simple, but powerful and direct, analytical tools for understanding the attitudes and behaviour of those with responsibility for managing others.

MacGregor argued that manager's assumptions about the attitudes and abilities of others colour their working relationships.

The left-hand columns in Tables 5.1 and 5.2 set out the Theory X and Theory Y hypotheses. The right-hand columns draw some practical implications from the attitudes.

Table 5.1 MacGregor's Theory X

Theory X managers think that people are:	Therefore, Theory X managers:
• indolent and do as little as possible • inherently self-centred and indifferent to the needs of the organisation • gullible and not very bright • resistant to change and lack initiative • lacking in ambition and prefer to be led	• have 'subordinates' and see them as part of the 'machine' • maintain close surveillance and punish mistakes • give detailed directions on how to conduct every aspect of work • make all the decisions • stress predictable outcomes and security above all else

Working for a Theory X manager is routine and repetitive.

It does not take a great leap of the imagination to see how these characteristics could be applied to some teachers and the way that they view learners. Learners in a Theory X teacher's classroom will have to endure excessive control, with the teacher constantly standing between the learning and the material because, in that teacher's view, individuals are incapable of making anything of the learning for themselves. Theory X teachers will have sympathy for surface learning approaches, valuing rote methods, the accumulation of facts and high levels of testing. There are fewer examples of pure Theory X teachers than there used to be, but the type is clearly recognisable.

Table 5.2 MacGregor's Theory Y

Theory Y managers think that people are:	Therefore, Theory Y managers:
• capable of development and it is the responsibility of the manager to direct them towards high personal objectives • keen to succeed and want to improve • likely to find self-fulfilment in their work • not by nature passive or resistant to change – they have become so because of their experience in organisations • capable of striving to achieve their own goals by directing them to organisational objectives	• respect individual rights and have 'colleagues' • allow others to learn from their mistakes • allow others to work in their own ways • seek change and improvements from all • understand what individuals want from their jobs

Theory Y managers look for ways of making work interesting and rewarding.

Theory Y managers sound like the kind of humane teacher we would all like to be. Unfortunately, it is not always possible to live up to the ideal.

Stop and think: Are you a Theory X or a Theory Y teacher?
Very few people will be extremes of either type. Where do your instincts lead you? Where would you locate yourself on the continuum below?

Theory X   Theory Y

- Can you think of people you know who are examples of each type?

- Does the concept of the Theory X and Theory Y manager/teacher match your intuitions?

- Can you think of specific situations where your reactions are characteristically Theory X or Theory Y?

The process of change

Teachers, as mentors, expect to make changes in the behaviour, attitudes and intellectual capacity of learners. How is this to be achieved? Very few teachers have a model of how they can intervene in the learner's journey to promote or sustain change.

People in general prefer not to change. Fear of change may be a result either of fear of success, or of fear of failure. In school, success in examinations just means more of the same, and in addition the learner may become a target for the envy of others. As a disincentive, this is more difficult for teachers to appreciate than the straightforward fear of failure.

The model of change management described below reflects a Theory Y approach to personal development. It assumes that human behaviour is complex and unpredictable, but nevertheless essentially co-operative and responsive. A second assumption is that there is some level of motivation on the part of an individual to make a change. Attempts to impose changes can, of course, be successful, but the most effective and productive changes to behaviour come about as a result of individuals being, at least, compliant.

However, willpower alone is rarely enough to bring about change. For example, it may be necessary to offer alternatives that meet the needs of the individual more directly and have an immediate pay-off. There may also be a need to put in place structural changes that facilitate changed behaviour.

Although the process of change itself is complex, with individuals experiencing disappointments, hesitations and relapses, the steps themselves are quite straightforward. Each stage is set out in the flow chart on page 78 and in Table 5.3 opposite, along with possible strategies the teacher, as change agent, can use.

Table 5.3 Stages of the change process

Stage	Strategies
1 Not interested in change May never have considered the need for change. Complacent about current situation and levels of performance.	This stage may be equivalent to the 'ordinary world' of the learner, and is sometimes known as 'unconscious incompetence', since the person needing to change previous patterns of behaviour may not be aware that change is necessary. The teacher as change agent may supply information or identify problems by asking '*I see your performance this way … Is that how you see it?*'
2 Thinking about change Learners may be stimulated by a teacher, friends or resources to take an interest in a topic, or they may have heard about a new way of working.	This may be equivalent to 'the learning impulse' stage of the Learner's Journey. The change agent can: • build trust • show empathy • point to development paths.
3 Preparing to change At some stage, the individual must perceive that the benefits of change outweigh the costs.	This may be equivalent to 'crossing the threshold' in the Learner's Journey. The change agent helps by facilitating new knowledge or stimulating changed habits.
4 Making changes Once learners have made a resolution to change, they may require more specific support. It may be necessary to change more than one aspect of work.	This may be equivalent to the 'trial and errors', and 'allies and enemies' stages of the Learner's Journey. The point has now come where mechanisms for supporting change should be put in place. These might be: • forming groups of like-minded people • arranging to work with a 'critical friend' • offering attractive alternatives to previous methods of working • encouraging 'visioning' • devising an action plan with the individual.
5 Maintaining change New techniques or ways of working become routine as learners achieve the reward for the effort they have made.	This stage may be equivalent to 'tests and examinations' and 'rewards and recognition'. The need here is for continuing support from the teacher and reflection by the learner. One useful technique is the use of a diary to monitor changes and record achievements. The new way of working should continue to be made attractive and advances should be rewarded.
6 Relapsing The individual may begin to move back to previous patterns of behaviour. This may be caused by lack of initial success, or other pressures; for example, as a result of negative pressure from home or friends.	This stage may correspond to a 'refusal of the call'. It could happen at any time in the cycle of change. There will be signals that old habits are returning. These should be recognised and acted upon. The structural dimension should continue to support the new ways of working.

An individual may move backwards and forwards between the stages, and spend varying amounts of time at each one. Knowing when someone is ready to move forward is a matter of judgement, which many teachers deploy instinctively.

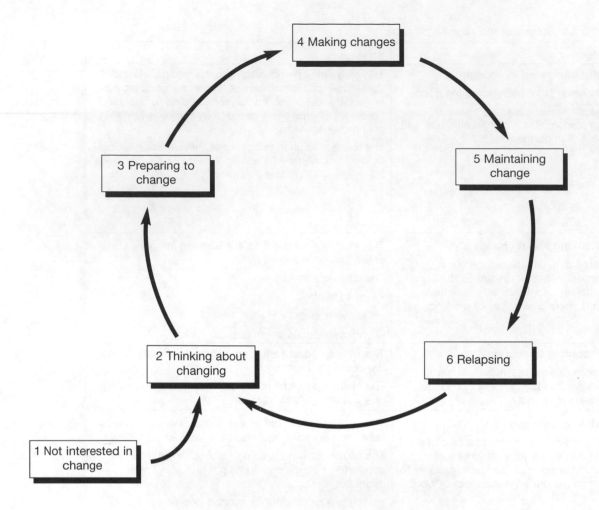

The process of change does not imply that an individual should completely abandon previous practice. Unless the circumstances in which change is required are extreme – for example, where failures of safety procedures directly threaten life – some maintenance of previous behaviour is probably desirable. In addition, to suggest that a complete change is necessary may be damaging since it implies that previous work was wholly unsatisfactory.

However, this kind of planned continuity is very different from a relapse, where previous undesirable patterns of behaviour begin to re-emerge. This may occur because of:

- personal circumstances (pressures in the individual's personal life militate against continuing with the initial effort needed to make changes)

- peer opposition (friends, often those with prestige, offer negative opinions; these are frequently expressed with damaging cynicism)

- perceived failure of the new behaviour (things do not 'come right' at the start and the learner loses heart).

WHAT CAN TEACHERS DO?

The main problem that teachers should be aware of is the possibility of relapse. This awareness involves:

1 recognising the early warning signs

2 anticipating some relapse and being prepared with ways of countering the problem

3 putting the whole process into perspective by pointing out how much has already been achieved and asserting that the process is not an 'all-or-nothing' issue, but a question of degree – do not allow a 'lapse' to become a 'relapse'

4 offering counselling for personal problems, or referring the individual to someone who is better qualified to counsel him.

Stop and think: How can you apply the 'process of change' stages outlined above? Does the model of change set out above reflect your own intuitions? How can it be customised to your needs?

Comment
You might gain a deeper understanding of the model of change by applying it to yourself and your colleagues before trying to analyse the position of learners. Consider the positions of at least three colleagues who are at different stages of the change process. What are the signs that identify the stages they have reached at the moment? If possible, you should particularly look out for people at the 'not interested in change' and the 'relapsing' stages. What could be done to move them on to a further stage in development?

Moving learners forward

Some learners respond well to the technique of discussing their current reality and then outlining where they would like to be. They like the kind of exercises on visioning suggested in Section Three (see page 45).

For others, any explicit discussion of developing a vision of themselves will be remote. The teacher must therefore exercise some tact, but a straightforward representation, such as the one given below, may appeal to those with a more practical turn of mind.

Set out overleaf is a Johari Window. Its purpose is to provide a simple, visual form that can represent the process of change. As a device for reviewing current positions and projecting future action, it can be used either as a medium- or long-term planning tool.

1 Where am I now?	**2 Where do others think I am?**
3 Where do I want to be?	**4 How am I going to get there?**

Learners should use the first cell to establish their current position. The second is there to provide a reality check – completion of *'Where do others think I am?'* may require either an increase or a reduction in an individual's estimate of her personal standing, since there are those who are over-optimistic and those who are excessively gloomy. Many learners will be unnecessarily pessimistic about their abilities and life chances. Learners should be encouraged to be realistic, and not talk their perceptions up or down.

The third cell represents the future. Although the cells are numbered in a certain sequence, they need not necessarily be completed in the order given. Some individuals may prefer to complete *'Where do I want to be?'* before any of the others.

The last cell, *'How am I going to get there?'*, leads naturally to the creation of an action plan for change. An action plan should be negotiated, and should represent a balance between aspirations and reality. Set expectations too low and the learner will live down to them; set them too high and the learner may wilt under unreasonable pressure.

Action planning

Action plans are a useful device for turning something quite abstract into a practical programme for achieving objectives. A good action plan should consist of:

● the overall vision of what is to be achieved

● objectives that are challenging, realistic and limited in number

● targets that specify what is to be achieved, and milestones that indicate an appropriate timescale

- the outcomes that the change is expected to bring about

- space for the individual to comment and review progress

- any provision for co-operating with others.

Action plans create circumstances in which individuals are accountable for outcomes. If the goals are clearly defined, and the individual is not coerced into agreement, an action plan represents a kind of contract – the kind that learners are more and more likely to encounter in their working lives.

Stop and think: Can you apply the propositions about change management to yourself?

Consider any aspect of your own life that you think requires change. This may relate to fitness, diet, habits, attitudes, personal characteristics, and so on. Make sure that, at least for the purposes of this activity, your choice is one that can be easily achieved.

- Identify where you are in the stages of the process of change (page 76–8).
- Draw up a Johari Window for yourself.
- Draw up an action plan to implement the change.
- Make it happen!

WHAT CAN TEACHERS DO?

1 'Crossing the threshold' is dealt with in further detail under the heading of *Inception* in Section Twelve, *Learning design* (see page 170). There are a number of techniques suggested there concerning pre-exposure and inception, which are directly applicable in the classroom.

2 Draw up a list of examination subjects. Ask each learner to write down their predicted grades for each subject. Ask them to add the job that they expect to do with that level of qualifications. Now ask them to write a second list, but with the grades lifted by one – so C goes to B, D goes to C, and so on. Now ask them to write down some jobs that *this* level of qualifications would open up. Ask them, is it really so difficult to raise grades by one level? Point out that moving up by one grade may be only a matter of two or three points.

3 Encourage learners to cross the threshold into new learning by finding examples of how new learning will make life better.

4 Find out about and communicate examples of how initial failures ushered in ultimate success. For example, some well known examples might include:

- Walt Disney being sacked by a newspaper for having 'no ideas'

- the Beatles being rejected in 1962 by a special team at Decca records with 'its finger on the pulse of youth entertainment' (five of the songs played at the audition went on to become top ten hits)

- Abraham Lincoln entering the Mohawk war as a Captain and coming out as a Private.

SUMMARY

◆ INCEPTION IS A KEY STAGE IN DESIGNING LEARNING.

◆ THEORIES OF CHANGE MANAGEMENT CAN HELP
TEACHERS TO UNDERSTAND THE PROBLEMS
EXPERIENCED BY LEARNERS AT THIS STAGE.

◆ A MODEL OF CHANGE MANAGEMENT CAN GUIDE
TEACHERS' ACTIONS.

Trials and errors

> In Section Six we learn that:
>
> ● There are a number of different contexts that teachers use to deliver learning.
>
> ● These contexts should be informed by explicit principles.
>
> ● While motivation is specific to the individual, there are some well-established strategies for teachers to try.

BACKGROUND

This Section, with Section Seven, divides the 'Tests, allies and enemies' step of the original Hero's Journey into two distinct phases: 'trials and errors' and 'allies and enemies'.

On the road, the hero undergoes a series of tests and encounters a succession of allies and enemies. In *Star Wars*, Luke and his allies have a number of adventures before attempting to rescue Princess Leia from the Deathstar. King Lear is tested by his experiences on the heath, while only a few of his 'loyal retainers' – including the Fool, an archetypal trickster – remain faithful.

Enemies seem to understand the rules of the road, while the hero is still learning. This puts heroes at a disadvantage, but they rapidly learn what they need to know. Making errors is an important part of this step. As long as the hero learns from them, the errors are a way of advancing progress. King Lear fails to learn from his errors, and ends tragically. The mentor may accompany the hero and act as a guide, or the hero may have to rely on the mentor's words of advice or a set of rules.

The hero's encounters give rise to greater understanding. The hero begins to realise that his quest entails a growth in self-knowledge as well as the completion of an external task. Indeed, the hero rapidly comes to the realisation that it is the inner quest which is the more important.

APPLICATION

For teachers, this phase has particular significance. 'Tests, allies and enemies' may be compared to the development phase of learning. Most teachers would agree that it is here that a significant proportion of their skills and talents should be deployed. Consequently, this step is considered in greater detail in the Learner's Journey. Formal examinations represent only one of the ways in which learners may face trials and make errors in school. For that unfortunate minority subject to bullying, merely turning up at school every day is a trial that requires immense reserves of courage. For others, the struggle to balance the demands of school with external attractions is a test of willpower. How can the teacher as mentor facilitate the progress of the learner through these stages?

A learning framework

The first step is to clarify a simple set of guidelines that can be used when planning and delivering learning. These include:

- **learning principles**

  All teachers operate with a set of implicit and explicit principles that guide their actions. Which ones do you hold to be important?

- **learning contexts**

  When delivering learning, most teachers will opt for whole-class teaching. This style is tried and trusted, but is it invariably appropriate, both to the learners and to the material to be delivered? What about other contexts, such as one-to-one, small 'seminar' groupings, and classroom-based group work itself?

- **learning design**

  Most teachers acknowledge the importance of designing learning so that lessons have a beginning, a middle and an end, but how many of your lessons simply end when the bell goes without having worked towards a distinct conclusion? When lessons simply run into the sand like this, learners frequently experience an undefined and uneasy lack of closure. The issue of learning design is considered in detail in Section Twelve (page 169).

Learning principles

Look carefully at Table 6.1.

Table 6.1

Principle	Description
individual accountability	Too often learners enter the classroom expecting to be 'fed' or to 'hitch-hike' on the backs of their colleagues. Even the most able prefer not to think for themselves. Learners could take more responsibility for either the goal of the learning, the sequencing of the tasks to be tackled, the use of resources, the roles needed to enable the group to get the job done, or all of these.
co-operation	Research shows that people are more motivated and learn better when they have the chance to share their ideas and experiences with others. However, simply putting learners into groups does not ensure that this will happen. Sometimes, certain individuals dominate while others are content to let the rest do the work. There are simple techniques that can be deployed, which encourage each individual to contribute positively to group work.
visibility	*Before* they start their work, all learners should know: • what they have to do • why they are doing it • how long it should or could take to complete • what will indicate success • how they will achieve it • how they will be assessed.
safety	Our emotions are a major influence on what, how and how much we learn. Learners arrive at the classroom door with a 'history' of experiences, both good and bad, arising from their life within and outside the school. Feeling safe is relative, but teachers can do a lot to make learning in their classrooms a more positive experience for everyone, which still challenges everyone to achieve more.

Stop and think: What are your underlying principles?

● What can you do to instil a sense of individual accountability in your classroom? How can you balance this individualism with co-operation?

● How can you make learning more visible?

● Are you convinced that learners feel safe in your classroom? Can learners make mistakes without fear of being ridiculed?

Comment

Developing a sense of individual accountability is an essential first step in creating a learning culture in your classroom. It means, for example, ensuring that everyone has the time to develop an opinion, not just those who are confident, quick thinkers. Also, having developed an opinion, learners should be willing to defend it. This entails encouraging learners to feel safe in expressing a point of view.

Learners co-operating with each other may be called positive interdependence. This is a necessary balance to the singularity of individual accountability. Teachers usually promote co-operation through group work, though this is often casually organised and lacking in rigour.

Learning contexts

Section Seven (page 99) suggests a more rigorous approach to organising work in groups, and provides ideas for developing individual accountability, but for now consider the contexts in which learning happens. Look carefully at Table 6.2. (Remember that learning may take place in a context that is a combination of those described.)

Table 6.2

Learning context	Description	Points to consider
one-to-many (whole-class teaching)	Presentations to a large group are the norm in many classrooms. However, they are often over-used and sometimes not very well delivered.	Used well, whole-class teaching can be stimulating and dynamic. However, too often it can be a passive form of learning. 'One-to-many' teaching may be most useful in passing on information, but it has limited value in changing attitudes, promoting problem solving or developing creativity.
one-to-one (see Section Five)	This is a more important learning context than many teachers realise. It can be used in mentoring and coaching as well as in guidance interviews.	It is very easy to confuse the forms of one-to-one teaching. Unfortunately, the main use of this technique is for reprimanding.
one-to-group (teacher leading a small group of learners)	Rather than conduct one-to-one interviews, it can be time-saving and more effective to conduct the same session with 4–6 learners.	Teachers can dominate these sessions at the expense of input from learners.
group work (learners work semi-independently of the teacher – see Section Seven)	This is where learners work together to solve problems and/or extend their competence.	The formation of groups requires careful thought relating to their size, composition and tasks.
through resources (for example, using textbooks – see Section Seven)	This is the use of independent learning resources. These can be completed on-site, at a distance, or both. They can utilise paper-based materials and/or new technology. They can be learner- or teacher-managed.	Developing your own quality resources takes a lot of time. Bought-in resources, however, seldom meet your requirements exactly, and so have to be adapted.

Teaching one-to-many (whole-class teaching)

The image of the teacher standing up in front of learners and talking to them is familiar to everybody. It is the way that most of us were taught and is the model of teaching most likely to be encountered in schools. Its greatest benefit to learners is for setting the scene, transferring information and reviewing a topic. It allows the teacher to launch a lesson effectively and focus on the subject to be learned. These benefits indicate why whole-class teaching is a vital part of any teacher's repertoire of skills.

Stop and think: When is whole-class teaching appropriate?
How do you react to the points below, which are frequently made about whole-class teaching? They are paired to illustrate how any approach needs to trade off the advantages with the disadvantages.

In whole-class teaching, the teacher:
1 **a** dominates every interchange
   b but can offer immediate feedback on learning
2 **a** directs the questioning
   b but makes systematic use of the board
3 **a** frequently degenerates into monologue
   b but can give spirited and charismatic insight into learning.

Comment
There is nothing wrong with teachers being in control and mediating learning. Learners in schools are, by definition, inexperienced and usually grateful for someone to guide them through the process. However, whole-class teaching at its worst can be dull, dispiriting and remote. Teachers who have a preference for this style do tend to dominate every interchange. Learners rarely talk directly to each other – everything flows through the teacher. If a response is slow in coming from a class, teachers frequently answer their own questions.

In talking about a topic, a teacher will clarify and reinforce her own knowledge. It is certainly true that the best way of learning a subject is having to teach it. Unfortunately, if whole-class teaching restricts the opportunities of making that breakthrough to understanding because only the teacher speaks, then the learners are being deprived of an important opportunity.

Individual teachers must work out their own formula for a successful teaching style. Such a formula will need to balance the teacher's talents with the needs of the learners and the optimum method of delivering the course content. However, it is very easy to adopt a one-dimensional approach, particularly if it plays to a teacher's strengths. Perhaps teachers who use the whole-class approach excessively should also question whether they are genuinely imparting knowledge or adopting a control mechanism – it is much easier to regulate a lesson if you are standing at the front with everyone expected to pay attention and look at you.

The truth is that no-one knows how much time should be devoted to whole-class teaching as opposed to any other style. Standing up in front of a class and speaking is what teachers do every day, but when shown a video of themselves at work, teachers are frequently shocked that they talk so much. Perhaps they should be more shocked that they sometimes talk to so little purpose.

Habitual use of whole-class teaching can lead to complacency and a slow erosion of concern for the necessary skills. Typical danger signs include:

- re-using material from previous years without any revision

- forgetting whether you have related a particular anecdote to a group or not

- individuals or groups anticipating your favourite jokes in a particular lesson (often because older brothers or sisters have warned them of what to expect)

- teaching while sitting at a desk

- never feeling apprehensive about how well a lesson is going to go.

The critic Kenneth Tynan once memorably defined the appeal of Laurence Olivier as lying in the sense of danger that he generated. Audiences felt, when Olivier was on stage, that anything could happen. The daily round of teaching makes it difficult to generate such excitement, but there should be occasions when a teacher's intensity of preparation matches that of an actor. On such occasions, there should be a consideration of:

- the vision you have of yourself as a successful communicator

- the effect you want to have

- the audience for your lesson and what stimulates their involvement

- the important effect that small details can have

- the value of enthusiasm, even passion

- the use of a wide range of reference to nourish the quality of your ideas.

The next step is to focus on the material and the teaching context. Begin your preparation with two simple questions:

- *'What do I have to convey?'*

- *'How am I going to get it across?'*

From these considerations flow others that will have a greater or lesser significance depending on your individual circumstances:

- *'Where will the learning take place?'*

- *'Do the learners have any special requirements?'*

- *'How long have I got?'*

- *'What has worked/not worked for this group before?'*

WHAT CAN TEACHERS DO?

1 Watch and learn from anyone who speaks successfully in public, such as actors, television presenters, politicians, and so on. What can you learn from them?

2 Occasionally, imagine yourself speaking to a group – visualise yourself as a persuasive and successful speaker.

3 Avoid self-indulgence (especially when relating anecdotes), insincerity and 'phoniness'.

4 Don't be afraid to use notes to prompt you during a long presentation.

5 Slow down from your normal speaking pace.

6 Vary the tone and pitch of your voice.

7 Avoid excessive use of expressions such as *'mmm'*, *'ahh'*, *'you know'* and *'alright'*.

8 Use gestures selectively as a visual aid; try to use your hands to paint pictures for the group.

9 Finally, for the bravest, make a video of yourself teaching crucial lessons. You can use this to analyse your own techniques, but you could also make the tape available for absentee students or for revision at the end of the year. (See *Learning from others: critical friend*s, page 96.)

Other learning contexts

Further consideration of the various contexts for learning (see Table 6.2 on page 86) leads to a consideration of:

● **cohesion**

The 'chemistry' of a group is mysterious. Sometimes, learners have very few problems in working together; at other times co-operation appears impossible. Nevertheless, teachers will want to employ friendship groups, ability groups and common interest groups to facilitate learning. The elusive quality that enhances learning for group members may be identified as cohesion.

● **access**

Access may be interpreted in a number of ways, from the simple level of *'Can everyone see and hear me?'* to the more complex issue of how to make the material understandable to a wide cross-section of the ability range.

● **differentiation**

If cohesion is concerned with groups, differentiation raises issues surrounding the needs of the individual. In any group there will be a wide range of ability. How does the teacher cope with this? The standard response is to pitch material somewhere towards the middle of the ability range, but there are other possible strategies. Teachers could differentiate by:

1 varying the speed at which they require learners to progress

2 supplying additional resources to the more able, or to the less able, as appropriate

3 setting different tasks for different levels of ability.

- **choice**

  Learners can sometimes exercise choice over the timing and sequencing of their learning. This is a matter for the structure of the course. Teachers can also inject an element of choice by setting a variety of tasks that require learners to make appropriate decisions. Not only is this frequently a good way of motivating learners, it also leads them along the path to autonomy.

Questioning technique

Clearly, a question should be framed to elicit an appropriate response. With careful planning, the exact wording of a question can be decided in advance, but generally the conceiving of a question should be left to the last moment so that it counterpoints the group's response to the material. However, framing questions may not be the problem. Most teachers would agree that the major problem is encouraging learners to respond to questions at all.

Set out below are some ideas for improving the ways that learners respond to questions. Open and closed questions have already been considered in the context of one-to-one interactions in Section Four (page 67). Those observations are still relevant in whole-class teaching.

Ideally, through appropriate questioning technique, the responses to questions should:

- make each individual accountable for their own learning (no 'hitch-hiking' in the classroom)

- be delivered in a safe environment (not one where individuals answering questions were subjected to howls of derision from peers, or withering criticism for mistakes from teachers)

- make learning visible.

However, as many teachers recognise, getting any response at all can be difficult.

WHAT CAN TEACHERS DO?

If you experience difficulty in eliciting responses from any of your groups, or if you are getting responses but want to try something different, vary the following tactics.

1 Tell the group you are going to ask them a question. You will then supply two answers: 'a' and 'b'. If they think that the answer is 'a' they should raise their hand with the thumb pointing upwards; if they think it is 'b' they should raise their hand with the thumb pointing down. If they do not know, they should keep their hand down, but they may be asked why they are not prepared to commit to one answer or the other.

2 Issue everyone in the group with red, green and yellow cards. When you pose a question, ask them to show a green card if they know the answer, a red card if they don't and the yellow card if they are unsure. This gives very visual feedback on the effectiveness of your teaching.

3 Ask a question and allow students to write down an answer. Then allow them time to compare their answer with the person sitting next to them. Finally, nominate an individual to answer.

4   Ask questions with your mark book or a class list in front of you. Tick the names of individuals who answer. Never nominate the same individual until everyone in the group has supplied a response of some kind over a specified period or set of lessons.

5   Nominate a 'response group' whose job it is to monitor the lesson and ask questions on behalf of the class. In the last five to ten minutes, they should summarise the main learning points and ask appropriate questions. Set a target for the number of questions, perhaps a minimum of five. You could even physically separate them from the rest of the group to emphasise their role. Naturally, you should rotate membership of the response group around the class until everyone has had a turn over a series of lessons.

6   Nominate an individual to answer a question before it is asked. Make sure that the question is easy, but do not fall into the trap of saying something like '*This is an easy one, even you could answer it ...*' and remember that as soon as you identify one person to answer, everyone else knows that they can hitch-hike.

Allowing time for answers

The time teachers allow learners to respond to questions is remarkably brief. It may be that the average waiting time for an answer to a question is as little as 0.5 to 1.0 seconds. Such speed is usually the result of a teacher's desire to pick up the pace of a lesson. This is admirable, as long as it does not become a habit that values only the rapid response. When the waiting time for an answer is extended to 3 seconds or longer with an explicit invitation to think deeply about a question:

- learners give longer answers

- learners give more adequate answers

- the number of '*I don't know*' responses decreases

- the number of hypothetical answers increases significantly

- the frequency with which learners ask questions themselves goes up.

Allowing more time to answer implies a change in approach. This includes:

- learning to live with the 'hanging' question

- asking learners to extend answers ('*Can you say a little more about that?*')

- seeing mistakes as opportunities (but move quickly to correct misconceptions)

- auditing how many times individuals answer questions in your lessons (see Section Ten, page 143)

- looking for the 'about to answer' learner and making encouraging noises or body signals.

Stop and think: How good is your questioning technique?

Monitor yourself with one class over the next few lessons. Investigate the questions below.

- What proportion of the class answers questions? How do you ensure that it is not the same individuals all the time?

- What kinds of questions do you ask? What proportion are open? What proportion are closed?

- How long do you wait for an answer? What happens if you extend the waiting time?

- How often do you ask for an extension or greater depth to an answer?

Comment

Clearly, there are issues of quality and quantity here. The number of learners that answer is a matter of quantity, while a consideration of open and closed questioning is one of quality. You may have found some difficulty in considering all the issues at once, and so perhaps preferred to set priorities. For Year 7 groups, the dilemma facing the teacher is usually how to select someone to answer without demotivating all the other willing hands, while for other years the problem may be how to galvanise apathetic learners into any response at all.

Motivation

As a mentor, the teacher's chief task is to maintain the morale of the learner. This involves some understanding of **motivation**. Unfortunately, most of us tend to think that what motivates us also motivates others. This can lead to confusion and frustration since it is rarely true. Even if we discover the factors that motivate an individual, they are likely to change over time. For example, research into what motivates people at work has shown that in their first few months in a job most are motivated by feedback on their performance; in years 1–5 they crave variety, autonomy and defined tasks; but pay, benefits and relationships with other workers and their supervisor assume greater importance after that (D. Katz and R. L. Kahn, *The Social Psychology of Organisation*, Wiley, 1966).

The same pattern may be true for learners in school. The new entrant to the school initially seeks reassurance and a safe environment, but rapidly moves on to valuing independence and variety. By the end of a school career, learners are more likely to be motivated by appeals to external success criteria such as examination results and show a preference for more adult relationships with teachers. We should also bear in mind that most teachers are products of a system that gives high prestige to a theorist learning strategy while only some individuals in the classes they face will share that preference. The challenge for the teacher is to find ways of motivating learners that are both effective and broadly based.

You may find the following 'rules' of motivation helpful, although you should remember that it will require a combination of these elements to motivate any one individual.

Motivation:

- is sparked off by people who are highly motivated themselves. There is nothing more likely to enthuse learners than for them to see you being enthusiastic. This does not mean that you have to be permanently ecstatic or change your personal style to a more active one, just as long as you show commitment to the learners and a genuine, personal interest in the material you are teaching.

- needs to be directed. Teachers need to set clear aims and objectives (see Section Three, page 50). Most learners like to work through a list of activities, which can be ticked off as they go along.

- needs to be constantly renewed. There is usually energy in abundance at the beginning of a new project or term, but do not expect that it will last. One of the areas in which teachers can demonstrate their creativity is in finding new ways to re-energise their classes.

- needs recognition. Everyone likes to feel that their work is appreciated. Although you might expect this to be so commonplace that it hardly needs stating, it is surprising how seldom teachers use recognition to motivate learners. Perhaps it is because teachers themselves manage on such a meagre diet of appreciation.

It is worth restating that the following all contribute to improved learner motivation and academic outcomes:

1 praise for good work that comes *soon after* the work is completed

2 praise that is detailed in its content

3 learners' work on the classroom wall. You may have other ways of recognising people's efforts. For example, many organisations now have an 'Employee of the week' plan – why not have a similar 'Learner of the week' scheme? Can you think of any other unusual ways of recognising good work?

- is stimulated by participation (the 'Hawthorne Effect'). The Hawthorne Effect is named after a study conducted into work conditions in the 1920s. The selected workers improved productivity even when the work conditions were varied adversely; for example, by lowering the light levels at their work benches and removing rest periods. The results of the study demonstrated that the workers' morale was high because they had been singled out for special treatment and this made them feel valued. Relationships between themselves and their supervisors improved because the experimental group were allowed to develop their own pace of work. These factors contributed positively to improved productivity. The Hawthorne studies suggest that involvement can lead to improvements in work. 'Involvement' for learners may mean some control over the order in which topics are tackled or participation in setting objectives under the guidance of the teacher. Involvement of this kind will stimulate effort, but remember that it will not last.

- needs progress that is observable. The setting of aims and objectives is part of the process of giving direction to learning. They also provide a yardstick by which to measure progress. The next step is to give learners regular feedback on the extent of their success. Reporting, whether formal or informal, is part of the process of keeping people involved.

- is stimulated by a realistic challenge. It is pointless and demoralising to set groups or individuals objectives that they have no hope of achieving. Challenges that are seen to be fair can help to raise standards, but balancing realism with rigour is one of the greatest challenges for the teacher.

- is stimulated by group identification. This is sometimes referred to as 'team spirit'. As part of a group, the individual may be motivated by:

  1 a desire not to let others down

  2 feelings of embarrassment (they do not want to be seen to be less competent than other members of the group)

  3 enjoyment at having skills that complement the others

  4 a combination of all of the above.

As every teacher knows, each class will contain at least one individual who is not motivated by team spirit, group involvement or any other motivational device. She may react against the goals set by teachers and either simply refuse to comply, or appear to be involved but covertly undermine the work of the class. To overcome the objections of those who are averse, the outcomes must either offer high reward or very unpleasant consequences. Unfortunately, it is easier to create resistance and inertia in learners than it is to spur them into learning.

Stop and think: How can you improve your ability to motivate learning?
Can you make use of any of the factors affecting motivation listed above? Learn from those who seem to have the knack of motivating others. Who do you know who is a good motivator? Why? What is it that makes others want to do things for that person? Are the same techniques available to you?

WHAT CAN TEACHERS DO?

1 Set goals in co-operation with the class. If allowed to set goals for themselves, groups will often be more ambitious, and achieve more than they would have done if targets had been set by someone else.

2 Encourage learners to find appropriate role models and emulate them.

3 Make a collection of strategies commonly believed to motivate people. Try to think beyond schools. For example, some organisations have posters round the walls with slogans such as *'We need customers more than they need us'*. Could this be adapted in any way for use in classrooms?

4 Improve the *quality* of your praise. Instead of saying, *'You've improved this term,'* say *'You are now much better at analysing primary data and using it in your essays'* (as appropriate to your subject).

5 Reduce the number of occasions on which you use tactics that demotivate learners; for example, stop criticising minor details, when on balance you know you should be praising what has been done well. Most teachers know that they should praise three times as often as they criticise, but very few actually attain this criterion. Never sink to sarcasm and condescension.

6   Relate the material you are teaching to life outside the classroom. Occasionally use your own life as an example and talk to learners about how you were changed by your own learning. If you do not do so already, consider using personal goal setting as a way of motivating yourself.

High definition teaching

Good teachers operate on a continuum running from 'minimum', where they deliver an adequate lesson, to the 'ideal', where everything goes right and learners are completely absorbed. Somewhere along this line lies the 'optimum' lesson, which is the best that can be achieved in prevailing conditions.

Minimum   Ideal

Occasionally, a teacher will deliver a lesson that just hums with inspiration, purpose and energy. Sometimes it happens because of meticulous planning and exemplary delivery, but sometimes it just happens. The effect can be electric. You detect a quality of silence and rapt attention in the learners and you know that you have captured something – their imagination, intellect or consciousness – and made a difference in their lives.

Such moments are not common. Lessons like this are examples of what might be called 'high definition teaching'. Because of the drain on emotions and energy, these lessons need to be balanced with more prosaic instruction. However, there is no reason why we should not aim to reproduce the circumstances in which they occur and struggle to deliver them more often. In doing so, we move the 'optimum' mark further towards the 'ideal' end of the continuum.

What is meant by 'high definition teaching'?

First of all, the technical aspects of the lesson have to be right. This does not simply mean that equipment or apparatus must be working, although clearly this is a necessary condition if it is part of the lesson, but high definition teaching does not depend on any extrinsic factors. The teacher and the delivery are the central focus. The key features seem to be:

● complete mastery of the subject matter

● infectious energy and passion radiating from the teacher

● learning design that is appropriate to the subject matter

● detailed attention to preparing the ground for the learning experience

● an opportunity for the learners to participate in the process

● material animated by linkage to life outside the classroom (perhaps through personal anecdote)

● variety in teaching methodology.

However, the mere presence of these features does not guarantee that high definition teaching will occur. There is an element of mystery surrounding teaching of the very highest quality. Nor is the list exhaustive.

High definition teaching is demanding. It takes time to prepare and energy to deliver. Such effort may be difficult to sustain over an extended period. Therefore, high definition teaching should be used selectively.

WHAT CAN TEACHERS DO?

1   Make your own list of features that produce high definition teaching for you.

2   When you experience a lesson that really works, spend a few minutes noting down why you think it happened on that occasion.

3   Raise the issue of the high definition lesson with your colleagues and compare your experiences.

4   Know your limitations: at first, aim to deliver one high definition lesson each week. Find out for yourself how frequently you can work at this intensity.

Learning from others: critical friends

Observing and analysing what others do, and inviting them to watch you at work, are powerful ways of improving your own teaching. For most teachers, having someone else in the classroom is stressful. However, there are ways of reducing the anxiety.

Agreeing a means of providing feedback has to be the first priority. Observation and analysis without a goal or a framework can be unhelpful for both parties. The learning framework described in this Section is a useful starting point and learning design is considered in greater detail in Section Twelve (see page 169). Use these to help you formulate questions to ask and themes to consider.

Opposite is a suggested observation schedule. It represents one person's observations of a PSE lesson.

If you consider observation and analysis to be a valuable process you must find time for it to happen in a systematic way.

One way of taking the fear out of lesson observation is to use a video camera to record the teaching. There is no need to use any elaborate cutting or editing techniques: simply set the camera up in the corner of the room and let it run. Afterwards, sit down with a colleague and ask her to comment on what she sees. This is much less stressful than actually having another teacher scrutinising your work directly.

Teacher	A. N. Other	Subject	Health and safety
Number in group	30	Gender split	11♀ : 19♂

Room layout (indicate position of the teacher and each learner, the location of furniture, and so on)

		Teacher			
♀	♀	♀	♀	♂	♀
♂	♂	♂	♂	♀	♀
♂	♂	♂	♂	♀	♀
♂	♂	♀	♀	♂	♂
♂	♂	♂	♂	♂	♂

Resources used including handouts and visual aids

Individual activity cards – these were a good idea.

Photocopied handouts, which were not easy to read and had a lot of information.

...

Learning design element (see Section Twelve)	Time from beginning	Observations
Inception	2 minutes	Teacher stood outside the door to meet learners – handed them an activity card. Learners took cards, some reluctantly, and went to their seats. They completed the activity. Latecomers also got the cards.
Introduction	5 minutes	Used a white board to make the aims/objectives of the session clear. Asked some of the learners to identify success criteria that could be used as a measure at the end of the session.
...	...	...

Comments/key questions

Was all the information in your handouts relevant? Did you photocopy the sheets or was it someone else? Did you check the quality before proceeding?

What did you hope to achieve with the activity cards? What atmosphere were you trying to create?

Do you think everyone in the group understood the aims/objectives? How do you know?

Were you happy with the seating arrangements? If not what could you do to change them?

...

WHAT CAN TEACHERS DO?

1 This Section contains a lot of ideas and information. You will need time to reflect on the implications for you and your teaching. Take a few minutes to set yourself some priorities for action.

2 Whatever you decide to do, keep the learning principles (page 85) at the forefront of your mind. Analyse the concepts, and play around with them to see if they suit your personal ideology. Always consider whether your lessons:

● make participants individually accountable

● help everyone to share their ideas in a constructive way

● have goals and targets that are accessible to all

● give learners the security that enables them to make a full contribution.

● use the full range of learning contexts to further differentiation

● incorporate the learning principles into each context.

SUMMARY

◆ SUCCESSFUL WHOLE-CLASS TEACHING CAN STILL CONVEY A SENSE OF INDIVIDUAL ACCOUNTABILITY TO LEARNERS.

◆ MAKING MISTAKES IS AN ESSENTIAL PART OF LEARNING AND SHOULD BE VALUED.

◆ INFORMED AND COLLABORATIVE CLASSROOM OBSERVATIONS CAN BE A POWERFUL TOOL FOR PROFESSIONAL DEVELOPMENT.

Allies and enemies

In *Section Seven we learn that:*

● Teachers are the most important, but by no means the only, allies that learners will encounter.

● Enemies may include social, psychological and relationship problems.

● Overcoming enemies can be a positive experience.

BACKGROUND

'Allies and enemies' is the second phase of the 'tests, allies and enemies' step of the original Hero's Journey. Whereas Section Six was concerned with the trials of the hero, this Section looks at sources of support that she encounters as she undertakes her personal journey. This step is also characterised by the creation of teams that possess special skills and qualities, which sustain the hero on the quest.

In *The Wizard of Oz*, Dorothy meets not only allies in the shape of the Scarecrow, the Tin Woodman and the Cowardly Lion, but also a bitter enemy in the Wicked Witch of the West. They form a group around Dorothy that comments ironically on the notion of the 'special team', since they actually lack the qualities required to support her. It soon becomes obvious that each of Dorothy's allies is also on a journey. In helping them to reach their goals, she often acts as a mentor, using a mixture of encouragement, reassurance and personal optimism to inspire them. She frequently models the qualities – courage, emotion and intelligence – that they wish to acquire.

In many narratives, the hero does not recognise until too late who the real allies and enemies are. King Lear is all too ready to accept the glib declarations of Goneril and Regan, but fails to recognise the love and devotion behind the actions of Kent, the words of the Fool or the plain honesty of Cordelia. Such failures to understand the rules of the journey inevitably lead to disaster.

Once again, if heroes learn how to overcome negative forces, the experience itself becomes a positive one.

APPLICATION

After some further consideration of the teacher's role in supporting learners, this Section goes on to explore some of the classroom techniques the teacher can deploy in developing and using learning 'allies' in the form of other learners and resources. The use of group work is discussed in order to point out how the teacher can provide a context for using others to promote learning. Group work offers the ideal context in which to form 'special teams' for the learner's journey.

By the end of this Section you should have some answers to the questions:

- *'How can the teacher promote the use of classmates as learning 'allies'?'*

- *'How can the teacher extract more from the resources that learners encounter?'*

- *'How can learners be spurred into a more intelligent 'reading' of resources in promoting the 'deep' approach to learning discussed in Section One?'*

Enemies can take many forms. At a personal level, the individual may be assailed by feelings of inadequacy or a lack of direction. At home, the prevailing atmosphere may reinforce these feelings through negative criticism or simply a lack of positive support. Negative role models may make suggestions such as *'I never took any notice at school, and look where I am now'*. When the enemies appear, that is the time for friends to offer additional support.

The teacher as ally

We have already considered the teacher as mentor in some detail (see Section Four, page 55). However, there are other roles that may be more suitable for specific situations. Consider Table 7.1, which sets out the broad differences between three roles of tutor, coach and mentor.

Table 7.1 Roles of the teacher, as the learner's ally

Tutor	Coach	Mentor
helps	shares	co-learns
timescale is short/medium term	timescale is medium/long term	timescale is long term
gives supervised practice	explores problems and offers the opportunity to try new skills	acts as 'devils' advocate', listens and questions
analyses tasks, gives clear instructions	jointly identifies problems, creates development opportunities	links work and other parts of life
emphasises the need for standard, accurate performance	goal directed to improvement and creativity	emphasises the need for change and questions the status quo

adapted from *The Learning Company* by M. Pedler, J. Burgoyne and T. Boydell, (McGraw Hill, 1991)

Stop and think: Which role do you prefer?

Consider the lessons that you taught last week. Did you adopt the roles of tutor, coach or mentor?

Do you think that greater awareness of the roles will help to improve the quality of your teaching? Are they incompatible?

Comment

You probably concluded that the roles are in fact contiguous; that is, a teacher may well begin acting in one role, perhaps as a coach, and then move on to another as the relationship with a learner develops. In each role, the teacher is acting as an ally. However, remember that the teacher may also be seen as the shadow by some learners.

Learning structures

Sections Four and Six discussed some of the contexts for learning, including one-to-one and whole-class teaching. We now turn our attention to working in groups.

We have already considered some issues concerning the formation of groups. For example, groups composed of individuals who have similar learning strategies may not function efficiently (see page 11). Another concern is that we tend to speak in very broad terms about 'groups' as though we know instinctively what they are and how they operate. In fact, teachers possess a rather poor vocabulary for discussing group work.

Set out on the following pages are some suggestions for five simple learning structures. You may find that you use them already, but have never considered that they need to be defined. If this is so, at least the names given to them will provide a basis for discussion with other teachers.

Think–pair–share

In this activity, learners are asked a question or posed a problem, which they have to think about first on their own, possibly making written notes. After a suitable period of time (usually only a few minutes) they then have to link up with another learner to share their ideas.

Use 'think–pair–share' to provide opportunities to consider questions and issues that may be difficult for learners to express in front of the whole group. In this sense, it is a kind of rehearsal before 'going public'.

Duo's check

This is an extension of 'think–pair–share'. Having formulated their thoughts or opinions, the pairs of learners then compare their ideas or answers with another pair to extend their thinking. Each pair 'checks' its understanding with another.

Use 'duo's check' to deepen consideration of an issue and as a route to developing learners' ability to work in a group.

Numbered heads

Each member of a group is given a number. The teacher, not the group, then decides what role each number will fulfil. For example, the following are roles that enable groups to operate effectively:

- director (makes decisions about what to do, and by when)
- facilitator (helps to make clear how things need to be done; for example, perhaps ensuring that all group members stick to any rules that may have been agreed)
- motivator (keeps everyone going and staying on task)
- conciliator (tries to keep everyone working together).

The roles may be allocated at random, or according to preferred learning strategy. 'Numbered heads' also offers the teacher the opportunity to vary roles so that individuals have to work outside their usual learning strategy.

Use 'numbered heads' to provide a disciplined approach to group work. Make sure that you rotate the roles. Encourage individual accountability by randomly calling on one of the numbered heads to provide feedback to the whole class rather than allowing a volunteer to respond.

The three-step interview

This is a more complex technique and makes greater demands on communications skills. It works best with groups of four. If you have an odd number, then you can fill the gap, or adapt the technique to a group of three.

The teacher decides on the issue to be discussed or sets the agenda in some way. For example, suppose the group were asked to discuss attitudes to '*My most memorable holiday*'.

Each member of the group is given a letter – A, B, C or D. In step one, person A interviews person B; at the same time, C interviews D, using questions or prompts as a guide. In step two they reverse roles: B interviews A, and D interviews C. In both steps the interviewer will need to make a note of the answers given. Finally in step three, they report back to their group, *but* group member A must tell B's story, C must tell D's and vice versa. In this way, they are forced to concentrate on the details of what the interviewee has said. The rest of the group exerts 'pressure' to complete because they are listening to their own descriptions or explanations being reproduced.

Use the three-step interview to develop communication and group work skills. It is particularly useful for any kind of work that demands keen observation and an eye for detail.

Simple experts

This is an activity that demands first-rate classroom management skills from the teacher and advanced communication skills from learners.

Step one is to organise learners into 'home' groups of four or five and allocate each group member a topic or idea to research. This can be done by self-choice, drawing lots or by the teacher making a decision.

Step two involves the members leaving their 'home' group and coming together with members of other home groups to form an 'expert' group. The job of the expert group is to research the information needed to make each individual an 'expert' in that topic. For example, if the overall topic is the causes of the First World War, there may be expert groups considering the arms race, imperial rivalry, and so on. The resources for each expert group to read and discuss should be prepared in advance by the teacher. Learners must gather the information they need and then discuss their findings in the expert group before returning to their home groups.

In step three, after a period of time determined by the teacher, and having become 'simple experts', learners should return to their home groups and represent their newly acquired expertise. In answer to the question *'What was the main cause of the First World War?'*, for example, each group member would present his findings, and it is then up to the home group as a whole to come to a conclusion.

This distinction between a home group and an expert group is a useful one because it encourages participants to be individually responsible for what they do. It helps to avoid 'hitch-hiking', where some rely on others to do the work for them.

Stop and think: On what occasions might each of the work forms be appropriate?
Of the five work forms described above, the first three are relatively simple to implement, while the communications skills demanded in the last two make them complex. Think back over your teaching last week: Where could you have used any of the work forms? Could you make adaptations to them, to suit your needs better?

Which do you think would be an appropriate form to follow up the last homework that you set?

Comment
Most teachers want a quick and direct follow-up to homework, so in most cases 'think–pair–share' is the right form. You can use it to check for errors before work is handed in or to consider answers to a question you may have set.

The ideal group size for classroom work is between two and five. Any more than five and more reticent learners find it almost as difficult to contribute as in a whole-class setting. Some suggested optimum numbers are set out below.

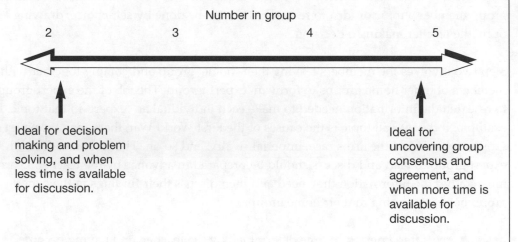

Number in group

| 2 | 3 | 4 | 5 |

Ideal for decision making and problem solving, and when less time is available for discussion.

Ideal for uncovering group consensus and agreement, and when more time is available for discussion.

Determining appropriate group size is just as important as judging group composition. Friendship may be an acceptable basis for forming 'think–pair–share' or 'duos' check' groups, but for more complex work, such as 'simple experts' or 'numbered heads', consideration should be given to other criteria, such as a mix of learning strategies.

Resources as allies

After the teacher and other learners in the class, the next 'ally' to consider is the resources available for learning. The material that follows deals with the most commonly used classroom learning resources.

Visual aids

Visual aids come in a number of different forms, such as objects, photographs, slides, videos, flip charts and overhead transparencies. Each of these has techniques of use associated with it. For example, you may find the '1-6-6 principle' useful in improving the impact of overhead transparencies. The 1-6-6 principle indicates that you should:

- have no more than one main idea on each transparency

- express the idea in no more than six lines of text

- use no more than six words per line.

If you need to convey large amounts of information, such as extensive tables and charts, produce a supporting handout rather than trying to present them on a transparency.

You may prefer to produce hand-written transparencies if you find that word-processed ones are too time-consuming to prepare. Alternatively, you may want to develop a transparency as you explain a topic to a class. There is nothing wrong with a carefully produced, hand-written transparency, as long as you adhere to the 1-6-6 principle and avoid the common error of overcrowding, which leads to confusion for the learner.

One of the best ways of recognising achievement is to arrange displays of students' work on the walls. They can be time-consuming to prepare, but they stimulate learning and are appreciated by learners who take pride in seeing their work on public display.

WHAT CAN TEACHERS DO?

1 Check whether the transparencies you use in your teaching conform to the 1-6-6 principle.

2 To produce a more professional look, use frames to block out the light around your transparencies.

3 Ask for expert advice from the art department on how to display work to its best advantage.

4 Make sure that work on the walls is changed regularly – at least twice a year.

5 Do not simply put work on the wall and leave it there. Make the material active by looking for opportunities to refer to it in your normal teaching.

6 Try using 'enigma' wall displays. For example, for a Design and Technology display, you could prepare a large card with the words *Technology: What did they say?* on it, and below have a series of pictures or name cards that learners must lift in order to find out what is underneath. Under the name 'Commissioner of the US Office of Patents, 1892', the quote *Everything that can be invented has been invented* could appear; under a photograph of Lord Kelvin, President of the Royal Society, 1895, you could display his assertion that *Heavier-than-air flying machines are impossible*; and so on.

Television

Most of the time, when we watch television, we allow it to wash over us without thinking too much about what we see and hear. There is nothing wrong with using television as a form of relaxation like this and most people never bother to consider that they could watch in any other way. Having said that, television is frequently discussed and analysed, although such discussion is invariably limited to the content of the programme.

What strategies can teachers use to engage learners more actively in the process of watching when they use television as a teaching medium?

The key to getting learners to be active in their viewing is to 'make it strange'. This sometimes means disrupting the programmes in some way in order to jolt learners out of the customary passivity of most television viewing. To varying degrees, learners will resent this, so be prepared for an adverse reaction.

Set out below are a number of techniques that draw on the unconscious learning of television codes. Most learners have watched so much television now that they can predict what to expect when they hear certain kinds of music at the beginning. You may want to draw attention to this unconscious expertise as part of building learner confidence and pointing out how unconscious learning occurs. For example, you could try:

- **no sound**

  Play an extract from the programme without any sound. Ask the group to decide what the programme is about. Ask them to write an outline, or the script for a section of the programme. Play the whole programme again with sound, comparing their ideas with the original.

- **no pictures**

  Play an extract from the programme with sound only, and no pictures. Ask the group to decide what the programme is about. Ask them to draw the visuals for an extract (reassure them that drawing skills are not important). Play the programme comparing their ideas with the original.

- **prediction**

  Play the opening title sequence with sound and pictures. Ask the group to come up with a synopsis of what they think the programme is about. This is an excellent opportunity to draw out what they already know and use the knowledge of experienced members of the group.

or

  View the programme before showing it to the group and break it down into coherent sections. Show the programme one section at a time. Ask the group to predict what will be coming in the next section, then check the prediction.

or

  View the programme before showing it to the group and break it down into episodes. Show the episodes to different sub-groups in random order. Call the group together and get each sub-group to describe their section. Ask them to construct the programme and clarify what they believe to be the main points made. Show the whole programme to reinforce learning and check understanding. (You could use 'simple experts' described on page 103 as a way of organising this activity.)

- **key words**

  As an individual activity, ask members of the group to make a list of what they believe to be the key words used in the programme as they are watching. Compare lists when the programme has ended. Come to a group consensus on the key terms. Run a short test to ensure that everyone understands the words.

or

  Before learners watch a programme, prepare a list of the key words as a handout and ask group members to tick them off each time they are used (note: it is difficult for learners to cope with more than ten key words, fewer if the words are new to them). Ask learners what this tells them about the programme. Are the words used in exactly the same way every time? Test to ensure that everyone understands the key words.

- **no colour**

  Turn the colour off by manipulating the television's controls. Explain to the group that you are doing this to act as a reminder that their attention should be on the content of the programme. In some specific circumstances the lack of colour could be made into a teaching point. For example, at a very simple level, colour is significant in the wiring of a plug or in experiments in Chemistry.

WHAT CAN TEACHERS DO?

1　Look to other sectors, such as advertising, for creative ideas to vary the use of visual aids in the classroom.

2　Try adapting some of the techniques suggested above for other visual forms (for example, posters with the words removed, so that learners must supply the writing, and so on).

3　Decide that you will never show a television in the classroom without making it 'strange' in some way.

Handouts

The photocopier may be the single most important piece of equipment in schools and colleges. This is perhaps a controversial view, and there are of course specific items in individual departments that are essential, but in terms of the organisation as a whole, the photocopier is indispensable. This is because teachers have come to rely on it to produce handouts that can:

- supplement textbooks
- remedy specific problems
- direct learners to other resources
- guide thinking and learning
- offer differentiated assignments.

Each of these requires a slightly different format, but the structure for most handouts would include:

- title
- aims and objectives for learning
- resources learners will need or could refer to
- action plan
- introduction to the material
- learning content
- activities
- pre- and/or post-learning tests
- ideas for further activities or reading.

As far as possible, handouts should be word-processed, but this is not always practical. For example, a teacher may finish marking some work at lunch time and realise students he is seeing that afternoon need a handout that will follow-up on their assignments in a specific way. In this kind of situation, it is better to respond immediately rather than produce a beautifully word-processed document that appears long after the optimum learning moment.

Title

It may seem a little unnecessary to dwell on something as obvious as a title, but there are some considerations to be given to its wording and design that can affect learning. Titles promote the materials that follow and prompt learner expectations. The pattern of headings and sub-headings is also a guide to the learning. As an example, you may like to consider how the hierarchy of headings is used within the Sections in this book.

Aims and objectives

Writing aims and objectives is dealt with in Section Three (page 50).

Supplementary resources

When you direct learners to resources, be sure that they are:

- readily available
- appropriate
- varied.

Typical resources might include:

- textbooks (or parts of them)
- newspaper, magazine or journal articles
- audio or video tapes
- other people and organisations
- electronic sources of information (Internet websites or CD-ROMs).

Action plan

If you have the space, consider including an action plan on your handout. You could either set out the shape of the learning programme and the deadlines yourself or leave appropriate space and negotiate the learning with the students.

Action plans are a useful device for turning something quite abstract into a practical programme for achieving objectives. In the context of a handout, an action plan is simply a device for clarifying what tasks will be completed, and by when. It may look something like this.

	Task description	Date for completion
1		
2		
3		
...		

Introduction and learning content

The value of an introduction is that the new learning can be linked to what has gone before. The aims and objectives, action plan and introduction are all aspects of that key 'crossing the threshold' stage of learning.

The material that you want to convey can be organised in just the same way as the structures suggested in Section Twelve (page 169).

The style you adopt should be straightforward. The acronym KISS is often used as a reminder to 'Keep It Simple, Stupid'!

Remember to control language in handouts for:

- jargon (but remember that to master the intellectual content of a subject, learners must demonstrate their control of the language or the 'trade dialect' of practitioners)

- academic grandeur (your writing should be correct, but not be stiff and formal)

- textbook imitation (there is no need to be impersonal – the writer of a textbook does not know your students, while you see them most days)

- level (some word-processing packages include programs that indicate the reading age of the material you have produced, but treat these with caution – you know your students, so write directly for them).

When writing use:

- direct address

- short paragraphs

- varied sentence lengths

- a conversational tone, though not too familiar.

Activities

Try to include varied activities on your handouts. As well as written assignments, at various times suggest that learners should:

- make presentations or mount exhibitions
- conduct interviews
- summarise the results of a group session
- design posters or fliers
- search for information using ICT
- make audio or video tapes
- produce a diary or log of their activities
- try writing in different forms; for example, a sensational newspaper account in science (*'Class 9b Dissect Heart – Teacher Sought by Police'*), or graphs in English (for example, the peaks and troughs of action in the five act structure of a Shakespeare play)
- develop checklists to be learned
- use role-play and simulations.

Pre- and post-learning tests

Teachers are well aware of the need for assessment. There are a number of suggestions in Section Eight that could be used to test learning either before or after the content has been taught. The value of testing before your material is taught is that the results can be used as a bench mark for the amount of learning that takes place. Sometimes pre-testing can identify whether a learner or a group already has a strength and you can vary your teaching accordingly. Giving students a signpost by pre-testing, and perhaps asking them to map their own learning, is a valuable exercise in developing independence.

Further activities or reading

One of the most common ways of offering differentiated learning is to provide 'extension' activities. These may take the form of suggestions for further practice or alternative reading. This is an unsophisticated reading of 'differentiation', but it is a start.

Textbooks

The textbook is, and will probably remain, the central resource for most teachers. Most modern textbooks can provide all of the essential learning for a course of study and a range of assignments that will stimulate learners. However, many teachers feel textbooks alone can not satisfy every aspect of the learning programme and enrichment material is required. This is usually supplied by the teacher (see *Handouts* above).

Remember that some parts of textbooks that are no longer usable in their entirety may still have relevant and useful chapters, illustrations or exercises. Directing learners to these parts of old textbooks through a carefully constructed handout can be a valuable exercise for the development of independent learning.

Libraries

The library is an important resource in developing independent learning. Most teachers are aware of this and want to use the library, but find the practical difficulties insurmountable. For example, how do you supervise those sent to the library? How can you use the library when there is no full-time librarian and you must rely on the goodwill of another teacher who is timetabled in for a library lesson?

From another point of view, how do you cope with an individual or group directed to the library, who arrive with a demand for books on 'volcanoes' or 'space exploration', for example? Usually, there is disappointment because there is very little or nothing available.

One practical solution is to involve the person who runs the library (whether a trained librarian, a designated teacher or volunteer helper) in planning a scheme of work so that she is forewarned of the need for books on a particular topic and can prepare accordingly. This applies equally to the local library if you are going to ask learners to research a topic using this resource.

You can help to solve the internal problem of learners leaving class unsupervised by issuing each learner with a library enquiry form, signed by you. This acts as a 'lesson absence pass' to be presented if the student is approached by another teacher while away from your class. A typical form might look like the one below. To save teacher time, the learner should complete the form and then presents it to you for checking and a signature.

Library Enquiry

Date _____   Time _____

Nature _____

_____

_____

Key search words _____

_____

Teacher's signature _____

WHAT CAN TEACHERS DO?

1   Working with a colleague, use the checklist for handout structure set out on pages 107–10 to review the quality of the materials that you use.

2   Examine old and unused textbooks for useful material. Tear out usable sections and repackage them into plastic wallets, pasting a guide to using the pack on the outside.

3   Outline to learners the next topic you are going to teach, and involve them in searching for available information before the project or assignment is begun, using the library, Internet, and so on.

4   As a department, involve the school or local librarian in discussing your needs for the coming year or term.

SUMMARY

◆ TEACHERS NEED TO WORK TO REFINE THEIR VOCABULARY FOR DISCUSSING GROUP WORK.

◆ CREATIVE USE OF RESOURCES CAN TURN THEM INTO LEARNING 'ALLIES'.

Tests and examinations

In Section Eight we learn that:

● *Revision periods resemble the 'approach to the inmost cave' for the hero.*

● *Examinations represent a 'supreme ordeal'.*

● *Teachers can deploy creative approaches to both these steps of the journey.*

BACKGROUND

This Section runs together steps 7 and 8 of the original Hero's Journey, 'approaching the inmost cave' and 'supreme ordeal'.

The hero, having passed through the various landscapes of the journey, aided by a series of allies but hindered by dangerous enemies, now has to face the ultimate test alone. As heroes prepare for this ordeal, they make plans, organise, and arm themselves with certain powers. They may be given a talisman, which will help them through the coming ordeal. Indeed, the whole journey so far may be seen as a preparation for this moment with the period immediately before the ordeal as a time of final preparation. The special preparations are necessary in order to defeat the last of the guardians who control entry to the 'inmost cave'.

If heroes survive these steps, they gain the reward. This may be some physical object of value, knowledge that brings happiness and relief to others, or personal enlightenment. Afterwards, a hero may realise that the ordeal was not really that demanding and that there are other worlds to conquer now.

In *The Wizard of Oz*, the supreme ordeal for Dorothy and her friends is to bring the broomstick of the Wicked Witch of the West back to the Emerald City. They are captured and the Witch sets the Scarecrow on fire. In extinguishing the flames, Dorothy splashes water on the Witch, who dissolves.

Following a series of disturbing nightmares and a banquet at which he sees the ghost of Banquo, Macbeth decides to seek out the weird sisters who had first foretold his fate. To find them he literally approaches an 'inmost cave' where he secures what he takes to be an endorsement for his continued reign as king. But the information is equivocal, and reassurances such as that 'no man of woman born' can kill him, prove to be misleading.

The hero accepts the need to be put to the test and take the risk of losing an old self, while stepping forward as someone new. The parallel with preparing for, and taking, examinations is a strong one. The final threshold guardians who must be overthrown are the examiners. One of the last acts of the mentor is to encourage the hero to enter the skin of the guardians/examiners and see the world from their point of view. Whatever roles the teacher may have adopted up to this point, learner and teacher unite in this task.

In a society without many rituals that act as 'rites of passage', examinations at ages 16 and 18 stand out for us as turning points in young people's lives.

APPLICATION

For learners in school, this stage of the journey is represented by any period in which they prepare for and take a test or examination. The 'supreme ordeal' may be represented by GCSE or A level examinations, but any classroom test or end-of-year examination may be seen as a rehearsal. The classroom suddenly becomes the 'ordinary world' and the examination room is the realm of danger and challenge.

This Section begins by looking at preparations for the big occasion, and then goes on to consider the more prosaic round of classroom testing.

Examinations

Overcoming anxiety

Tests and examinations make people nervous. This tension may be viewed as part of the 'shadow' accompanying the learner on her journey. There is no way of getting around nervousness – indeed it may well be a good sign, showing that learners are in a high state of readiness and prepared to show what they can do. Instead of trying to pretend that it doesn't exist, most teachers wisely use learner anxiety as a way of focusing energy. For some people, however, this state of readiness can go too far and interfere severely with performance. Even the vast majority of learners, who simply feel that nerves might get in the way of them doing their absolute best, would prefer to have some techniques for minimising their effect.

So how can we help to reduce the effects of nerves? The answer is quite simple. The main reason that learners feel nervous is that they fear the unknown. Therefore, the proper response to nervousness is to reduce the number of unknowns that learners are likely to meet. This involves preparing learners thoroughly beforehand, so that they feel confident that they have a good grasp of the content they need to cover, and feel familiar with the style and surroundings in which they will be asked to demonstrate that grasp. The paragraphs that follow give some ideas of how to achieve this preparation.

One part of the challenge for teachers in preparing candidates for a test or examination is to motivate them to acquire, retain and apply the knowledge, skills and understanding they need for examination success. To help you to do this effectively, try to put yourself in their position.

Stop and think: How keenly did you feel examination pressures?
As teachers, we always feel for our candidates as they prepare for and sit examinations. But how deeply do we remember the feelings evoked? Have the years dulled the feeling of panic associated with this particular 'supreme ordeal'?

Comment
Consider for a moment the obstacles you face in empathising with examination candidates.
- *Your status. Your current job as someone preparing others for tests and examinations indicates that you were probably successful at passing them yourself. Always remember that your students may not be so adept.*

- *Your subject knowledge. You know your subject well (you practise it all the time) and probably like it. The learners in your classes almost certainly will not have your command of the material and may not share your love of the subject.*

- *Your territory. Schools and examination rooms are familiar to you. The examination room itself has a unique 'feel' with its long rows of desks, patrolling invigilators, 'notices to candidates', and time-bound, rule-governed atmosphere. Unfortunately, schools can rarely give direct experience of this until the actual examinations since such extravagant use of space is usually impractical for mock or end-of-year examinations.*

Consider also that:

- *some candidates will have illnesses, complaints and allergies, which will detract from their capacity to succeed*
- *some will be experiencing personal difficulties that will disrupt their plans.*

WHAT CAN TEACHERS DO?

1 Be prepared to undergo the alarm and dread of the inexperienced learner by occasionally taking a night school class in a subject completely new to you: A level maths for English teachers; a modern language class with an emphasis on oral communication for science or PE teachers; any subject which requires manual dexterity or physical skill for history teachers; and so on. The idea is that you should put yourself the other side of the desk and feel the insecurity of not being in control of the learning experience.

2 Watch out for the learner who displays excessive signs of nervousness before tests and examinations. Make sure that there is plenty of opportunity for him to become familiar with all aspects of the examination process.

Timing

Well in advance of the actual test or examination, write on the board or give the group a piece of paper headed *'How much time to the exam?'* and get them to work out how much time remains for revision. Use this as the starting point for developing a personal revision **timetable**, in which learners must integrate the demands of all their subjects. Remind them to build in time that is already committed elsewhere, such as a family holiday.

Priorities

The next step is to set **priorities** by working with learners to decide what they have to cover in the revision period. Teachers will probably want to give learners the topics, but should allow some leeway in deciding in what order they should be tackled. Priorities might depend on issues such as which examination comes first. For greater precision, ask the group to set out a chart like the one below. Tell them that they must use only two levels of competence (either 'good' or 'bad') and significance ('high' or 'low'). This avoids the fudge of 'OK' which does not really help. Teachers may need to use their experience to indicate the level of significance of some topics to the examination. However, as many decisions as possible should be left to the individual learner.

A typical competency review sheet might look like this.

Topic	My level of competence	Significance to the exam
digestive system	good	high
circulatory system	bad	high
...		

This should produce categories such as good levels of competence and high levels of significance, and bad levels of competence but high significance, and so on. Remember that this needs to be done well in advance of the examination to leave plenty of time for deficiencies to be remedied.

From this analytical work on timing and priorities, candidates should produce an individual action plan. Advise them that this plan should be in the form of a chart and be kept somewhere prominent such as on a mirror or on the back of the bedroom door.

Active learning

One of the most difficult tasks to accomplish when preparing learners for tests and examinations is to reduce the sheer volume of material to manageable proportions. Many learners adopt the strategy of simply reading through their notes or other material in the hope that it will somehow stick. This is not a recommended procedure. In preparing for examinations, the emphasis of revision should be on **active learning**. This means that material should be manipulated and transformed so that the learner feels ownership of it.

Consider the following method for helping learners to absorb a large amount of material. You could go through the method for one topic in class to demonstrate how it should be done. However, it is most important that learners do the rest of the work themselves.

- Take all the material to be learned and organise it into separate topic areas (if learners' notes are on file paper this should not be too difficult).

- If there are some pages with notes relevant to two topics, rewrite the overlapping material onto other pieces of paper so that it can appear twice without having to move paper from one topic to another.

- Taking one topic at a time, spread all the pieces of paper out in front of you, grouping them into appropriate sub-topic areas. This is probably best done on the floor, though a large table may be enough.

- Now take pages of notes that need to be learned and, on a separate piece of paper, rewrite each page into a single, brief paragraph that contains all the most significant items of information. The idea is to condense the material to more manageable proportions. Learners may need some guidance at this stage in selecting the most significant items.

- Now reduce the material even further by taking the paragraphs and, on yet another piece of paper, rewriting the most essential information from each paragraph into a single sentence. Alternatively, the distilled information could be drawn out in a logical and memorable way as a 'model map' (see *MapWise*, by O. Caviglioli and I. Harris, Network Educational Press, 1999). This should reduce the whole topic to one side of A4. Let's call this the 'master sheet'. This progressive reduction is not easy, but it can be done. The whole process may be represented diagramatically as shown over the page.

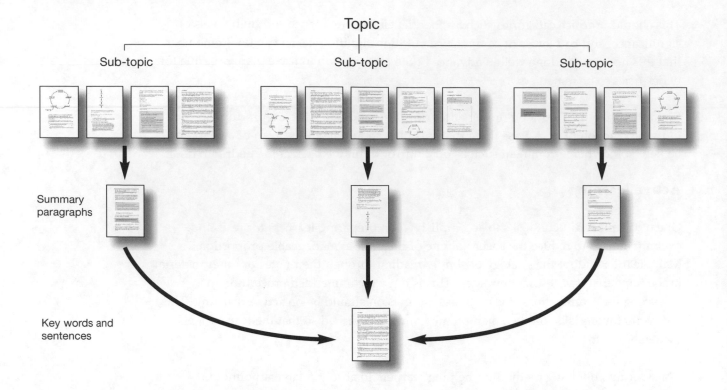

This process reduces the information to a manageable volume and creates pathways back from key words and sentences, to essential information at the paragraph level, to important areas of learning. The sentences and words on the single sheet of A4 act as prompts for the mind in recalling knowledge. The single side of A4 must now be committed to memory.

- As they condensed the information, learners will have already absorbed a considerable amount of material, but in order to be sure they should cover the master sheet and try to re-write everything onto another sheet of A4 from memory. In this way, learners confirm the links to the information to be learned. Only when they have got it perfect can they begin to feel some cautious confidence.

Some learners who use this technique go into a test or exam and write out the A4 page before they even look at the questions. Is this a valid technique for your learners?

Memory techniques

Suggested below are a number of ways to help learners remember the information they need. However, memory tends to be individual and the techniques suggested may not measure up to the needs or temperament of everyone. You might want to direct everyone to use at least one technique (for example, using a simple notebook) as a baseline, but suggest that they should try others individually, or in combination, until they find an approach that suits them.

Notebooks
The first technique is simply to suggest (or insist) that learners keep a small notebook with them at all times. It can be used to keep lists of items to be learned. Learners can refer to it on the bus, waiting at a supermarket checkout or at any other private moment! This is an excellent way of making use of time that might otherwise be wasted.

       Adventures in Learning

Audio recordings

Have you ever noticed that everyone seems capable of learning the words of popular songs and advertising jingles with ease, yet no-one ever seems to expend any effort on it? Partly this is because they are written to be catchy, but it is also because they are repeated so frequently. Learners can make use of this technique. Encourage them to make an audio recording of the points they need to remember and replay it whenever they have the opportunity. If they can make the information catchy in some way, using the models of popular songs or advertising, then so much the better.

Changing the form

Learners should try to transform the information they have to learn in some way. For example, they could turn written information into a graph, or rewrite a piece of dry information into a series of sensational newspaper headlines.

Brain imaging

There are many names for 'brain imaging': it is a well-established memory technique. It is particularly useful if there is a large amount of information that has to be memorised in a sequence. Learners should:

- consider the list of items to be remembered

- think of a location that they know well (for example, their own bedroom or a route they travel regularly)

- link the items to be remembered to the location by mentally placing the items around the room (perhaps sweeping from right to left) or along the route – for example, *'I'll put item A on the dressing table; B on the bookcase; C on the chest of drawers …'* and so on

- try to make the links memorable in some way by using colour or affiliating disparate objects – for example, *'I'll put the Duke of Wellington on the TV'*

- for different topics or lists, choose different locations.

When learners need to recall the list, it is a simple matter to 'go around the room' in their minds picking up the items they need to remember as they go along.

Stop and think: How can these ideas be adapted to your subject?
All the ideas set out above, on pages 115–9, are general in their application. How can they be adapted to meet the needs of your subject?

Past papers

If learners undertake the activities described above, they should be strongly placed to produce good answers in examinations. However, this is not enough on its own. They must also look at how they can present the information in the best possible way. Many teachers use past papers as part of preparing learners for examinations. This helps learners to judge the kinds of questions that they are likely to encounter. However, unless used creatively, past papers can be a very passive exercise.

Instead of simply setting a past paper as a kind of mock examination, create a mark scheme for the questions with the learners, and then ask them to mark the work of others, returning it to them with comments. They could even undertake the full process of setting questions, creating a mark scheme, marking the answers and suggesting grades. However, all of these stages require considerable skill, so treat it as a way of helping learners understanding the mind of the shadow/examiner.

Examiners are usually very precise about what they want from candidates. For example, if a question asks candidates to list a number of items, they will not get any marks for going on to describe the items. Similarly, candidates in any subject with a mathematics element should be very careful about the differences between 'sketching' and 'plotting' a graph.

Teachers can promote learner commitment by keeping an image of success constantly in front of their eyes. Use the ideas on creating a vision (Section Three, page 45) to remind candidates about how they can sustain themselves through the dark times by creating a self-image that focuses on success.

WHAT CAN TEACHERS DO?

1   Just before the examination, check that candidates are clear about the structure and requirements of the examination paper by setting them an exercise to create *'The examination paper I would like'*, with the full timing, rubric and pattern of questions (for example, *'two from section A; one from section B'*, and so on). They could use past papers to get help with the appropriate wording for questions. Ask them to exchange papers, once completed, and check each other's ideas.

2   Undertake a visioning exercise with your group. Ask them to imagine it is the last Thursday in August. They are opening the envelope that contains their results. Ask them to feel the thrill of seeing the list of grades that they want. Suggest that the grades are so good that they feel a little embarrassed about telling their friends about them and they have to be drawn out by discreet questioning. Ask them to hold on to that feeling.

3   Use past papers to build a stockpile of all the verbs learners are likely to meet in the examination and define each one. For example:

define   provide a generally recognised explanation

analyse   find the underlying principles, ideas or parts

describe   give an account in words

and so on.

In the examination room: focus and relax

Warn learners that they must pay attention to the rules of the examination room, but they should also be aware of their rights. For example, if they are uncomfortable in some way, perhaps sitting at a desk in direct sunlight, and feel this might interfere with their performance, they should say something to the invigilator. Similarly, if they are too cold they should ask for the heating to be turned up.

Rehearse with learners a routine for sitting at their desks. Everyone knows that it is important to sit properly. Learners should keep their backs straight and make sure that the backs of their legs are supported.

Suggest that, as they look through the question paper, they focus on their breathing to improve concentration and minimise stress:

● breathe in through the nose

● release the breath through a slightly opened mouth (as though whistling, but without making any sound)

● repeat three times.

Suggest that between questions they could use some simple exercises to relieve some of the physical tension that builds up in an examination. None of the exercises should attract the interest of the invigilator or disturb other candidates. For example, the sequence should not involve turning the head from side to side. The simple six-step programme described below should help. The exercises should be repeated about three times.

1   Reach forward and extend the fingers. Clench into a fist and extend again.

2   Slowly shrug the shoulders up and down.

3   Gently move the head from side to side as though trying to put an ear on the shoulders (do not roll the neck).

4   Gently nod the head so that the chin touches the chest, then stretch back.

5   Hold the head up, lean forward and gently arch the back inwards.

6   Put palms together between the thighs and squeeze inwards with the legs, against the hands pressing outwards.

WHAT CAN TEACHERS DO?

1   Get hold of a number of relaxation tapes and listen to the techniques that they suggest. Adapt them for the examination room and teach them to learners so that they can overcome the occasional feeling of panic that sweeps over candidates and convinces them that they can remember nothing.

2   Suggest to candidates that they should think of something that always makes them smile or feel happy. Good examples include a family pet, a place that they love or a relative who always tells jokes and generally acts the fool. Propose to learners that they should think about this 'talisman' whenever they are in an examination and feel too threatened.

Testing

The methods of testing explored below are:

- cloze procedure
- sentence completion
- sequencing
- multiple choice
- true/false statements
- labelling diagrams
- case studies and questioning.

The ideas for testing set out below are for the use of teachers who want a guide to how much learners have absorbed, but feel that their current repertoire needs extending. Remember that in administering classroom tests, the role of the teacher changes from mentor to threshold guardian.

More detailed issues of testing, such as standardisation, should be pursued through specialist literature.

Cloze procedure

Cloze tests are often used to test reading ability. A suitable text is chosen and then words are deleted. If the person setting the test wants to make it more difficult, every fifth word could be taken out. Easier tests might involve every tenth word being removed. The reader is asked to fill in the missing words by choosing from a given list – in this way her comprehension is tested.

Teachers can use a similar technique, but interest will centre on the words that are relevant to the learning programme.

Consider the following material on health and safety.

> Read the following text and use the words underneath to fill in the gaps.
>
> *Ingestion and injection injuries are fortunately rare in the workplace. Certain occupations, such as those associated with _____ , are more vulnerable than others. _____ , _____ and _____ and others working in _____ and _____ have to take special measures to reduce the risks. This is particularly true to prevent the spread of the _____ virus and _____ . Both types of injury generally occur when _____ standards are not met. The application of _____ , and of strict procedures, is the best risk prevention measure.*
>
> | | | |
> |---|---|---|
> | **nurses** | **hospitals** | **primary care practices** |
> | **hepatitis B** | **domestics** | **occupational** |
> | **health care** | **good working practices** | **doctors**   **HIV** |

The completed text should read as follows.

> *Ingestion and injection injuries are fortunately rare in the workplace. Certain occupations, such as those associated with <u>health care</u>, are more vulnerable than others. <u>Nurses</u>, <u>doctors</u> and <u>domestics</u> and others working in <u>hospitals</u> and <u>primary care practices</u> have to take special measures to reduce the risks. This is particularly true to prevent the spread of the <u>Hepatitis B</u> virus and <u>HIV</u>. Both types of injury generally occur when <u>occupational</u> standards are not met. The application of <u>good working practices</u>, and of strict procedures, is the best risk prevention measure.*

Unless you are directly involved in health and safety, you may have found this quite a difficult exercise. However, you can begin to make it easier by completing the words you are almost sure you can get right. For example, the word 'virus' would probably trigger the pairing of 'Hepatitis B' and 'HIV' for most people. The three blank spaces together would also suggest the sequence of 'nurses, doctors and domestics', though some might waste time agonising over which should take precedence in the list.

Once half the list has been allocated to the text, the remainder should be relatively simple. You may also have observed that:

- it might be confusing for some learners to have ten blank spaces in the passage, but be provided with a total of fifteen words in the list below

- taking out words at the beginning of a sentence is particularly confusing (for example, must a word that starts a sentence begin with a capital letter?)

- the better your language skills the more likely you are to pick up the grammatical clues

- two of the items – 'good working practices' and 'primary care practices' – are quite similar in wording, possibly leading to unnecessary confusion.

Despite these, and other, reservations the cloze test is a convenient way of checking whether learning has taken place. It has the advantage of being simple for the teacher to devise.

Variations on the theme include making the test:

- easier by giving learners the passage beforehand as part of the course material

- harder by not giving them the words to be put into the passage.

Sentence completion

For this kind of test, learners must finish a sentence that relates to the learning topic. The sentences used for this kind of test may come either from material that already exists or be devised by the teacher specifically to check on learning.

The completed part of the sentence may be either a single word or a longer phrase. Consider the two examples:

> - *Human skin comes into contact with many toxic chemicals in occupations such as*
>   _____
>
> - *Oozing, redness and thickening of the skin is called an*
>   _____

Notice that the first one is a relatively open question. Answers could include engineering, agriculture, chemical processing and others. There is room for some interpretation in the second sentence as well, but the limits are much more clearly set. The answer most commonly suggested is 'inflammatory reaction'.

Teachers who use sentence completion tests should be aware of the possibility of a wide range of answers, some of which may be right, but not exactly what you were looking for. How would you deal with this?

Sequencing

Sequencing exercises are good for testing learners' knowledge of processes or skills that have an accepted order of actions.

The teacher takes a description of the process or skill and cuts up the sentences, placing them in a random order. The task for the learner is to re-organise them so that they make sense. Once again, grammar clues may aid those who are more literate. Consider the following text.

> *The use of protective gloves is also strongly recommended. If the skin is exposed to damage, washing the point of contact with a stream of water helps to reduce injury. The risks of damage to the skin can be reduced by good hygiene practices. Barrier creams form a good line of defence.*

The original is as follows.

> *The risks of damage to the skin can be reduced by good hygiene practices. Barrier creams form a good line of defence. The use of protective gloves is also strongly recommended. If the skin is exposed to damage, washing the point of contact with a stream of water helps to reduce injury.*

Clearly, the writer felt that it made sense to begin with a general comment ('good hygiene') and then work outwards from the skin ('barrier cream') to 'gloves' and conclude with what to do if contact does occur. However, it is quite possible to organise the sentences in an entirely different way, make sense and still have grammatical consistency.

Teachers should be careful of setting texts that can be interpreted in a number of ways like this, or at least be prepared for learners to come up with unwanted answers that are still right.

Multiple choice

> *Tick the correct response to the question below.*
>
> *Multiple choice tests are best for:*
>
> *A testing skills*
>
> *B testing knowledge*
>
> *C judging attitudes*
>
> *D playing guessing games.*
>
> **(Answer: B)**

Multiple choice tests are difficult for the untrained person to construct. Anyone who has tried to set this kind of test will recall wrestling with the difficulties of finding answers which are possible, but not so close to the correct response as to be indistinguishable from it. They are also very time-consuming to construct. Unless you are particularly adept at this kind of test, they are best avoided.

True/false statements

These are simple to construct, but as a testing device they have the disadvantage of being unreliable because guessing may earn learners a high mark. For every item they have a 50% chance of being right. One way of overcoming this is to require a justification for an answer. For example:

> *Tick true or false:*
>
> *Exposure to chromium compounds can cause inflammation of the larynx and the liver.*
>
> *true/false*
>
> *This is because (justify your answer in full)*
>
> _____

Labelling diagrams

Where knowledge or a skill can be visually represented, a good test is to ask learners to label a diagram. Not only does this offer those with good visual memories a relatively rare opportunity to deploy their talents, it is also a change from other forms of testing, which are so heavily word-based. A variation is to give the wording of the labels, and ask for the diagram to be constructed.

Case studies and questioning

Most learners like case studies. They have the feel of genuine experience and learners frequently identify with the person who is the centre of the story. Most teachers have a store of anecdotes that they use to enliven their teaching. These are the raw material for case studies.

The writing should be simple, straightforward and short (500 words is usually more than enough). Like any story, it should be structured around a beginning, a middle and an end. There should be a point to the story. For example, it should illustrate good or bad practice.

After the case study, set questions to test learners' comprehension and also assess how far they can apply their own knowledge and understanding to the material. Questions should be both open and closed (see Section Four, page 67) – about 75% should be closed and 25% open, though the marks may not be allocated to the questions in these proportions.

WHAT CAN TEACHERS DO?

Remind learners of the '5Ps' Principle: **Perfect Planning Prevents Poor Performance**. Another slogan you might use is **Fail to prepare: prepare to fail**.

SUMMARY

♦ 'VARIETY' IS A KEY WORD WHEN PREPARING FOR TESTS AND EXAMINATIONS: THE APPROACHES AND MATERIALS SHOULD BE JUST AS VARIED FOR REVISION AS FOR OTHER ASPECTS OF TEACHING.

♦ 'VISIONING' IS A USEFUL DEVICE FOR LIFTING THE EYES OF LEARNERS FROM THE DRUDGERY OF REVISION TO THE FEELING OF ELATION THAT COMES WTH SUCCESS.

♦ CREATIVITY, COMBINED WITH METICULOUS ATTENTION TO DETAIL, IS THE KEY TO SUCCESS.

Reward and recognition

In Section Nine we learn that:

● Rewards and recognition take many forms.

● Teachers can promote learner autonomy in a variety of ways.

● Public relations and marketing are innovative ways of recognising success.

BACKGROUND

After the storm and stress of the 'supreme ordeal', the next step – the 'reward' – is a time of reflection and contemplation. The hero can savour the fruits of victory and consider the next phase of the journey. The hero has changed and something new has been born. Celebrations follow and there may be a 'debriefing' as the hero recounts the events of the ordeal to the mentor.

The hero may now have become a member of an elite group and success may entitle her to new rank and status. She may have acquired a desired object or special powers. However, the key to the hero's new understanding is the self-knowledge that she has attained. This inward and outward recognition of achievement gives the hero a new perspective on herself and her world.

A traditional reward for a hero was the hand in marriage of a princess following a series of trials set by an apparently implacable father, or father figure. In *The Tempest*, Ferdinand's reward, following the trials imposed by Prospero, is marriage with

Miranda. Increasingly, in modern narratives, the story line is varied to 'girl gets boy' as well as the more traditional 'boy gets girl'.

Rewards may also have a more practical benefit. In *Star Wars*, Luke and his allies not only rescue princess Leia, but also escape with the information about how to blow up the Deathstar. Unfortunately, this victory seems to be won at the cost of Obi-Wan Kenobi's life.

A secondary perception that frequently complements the reward, is the realisation that the opposing powers were not as formidable as they had initially appeared. This is certainly true in *The Wizard of Oz* where the apparently powerful wizard is revealed as weak and ineffectual.

APPLICATION

The reward for a learner at the end of a course may be paper qualifications, but to value this alone would be to miss the point of learning. The outward appearance of success, the symbolic representation, should not be confused with the personal reality of change and growth. By this stage in the journey, learners should have achieved some measure of success and that mastery gives them greater power over their own lives. This control is far more important than the outward trappings. What can the teacher point to as the best outcome of the educational process if the paper qualifications are relegated to secondary significance?

Most teachers would agree that ultimately they aim to develop individuals who are capable of learning for themselves. In doing so, they locate themselves within the tradition of liberal humanism, which has always emphasised the need to realise the full potential of each individual whether his talents are academic, creative, sporting or practical. However, in British educational thinking, individualism has usually been tempered by an acknowledgement of the need for group and social skills. Reconciling the needs of the individual and the group is a creative tension that has always presented a challenge for the perceptive teacher.

Independent learners

At the end of an educational process, what are the characteristics that we are looking for from an autonomous learner? If this is the reward that the learner can carry forward as a life-enhancing quality, what are the personal qualities we should be working to develop?

Characteristics of the independent learner include the ability to:

- **select appropriately from a range of learning activities**

    It is argued elsewhere in this book that learners should be offered a varied diet of experiences (for example, Section One). If we are serious about delivering variety, then learners should occasionally be presented with a choice as to how they get work done. 'Choice' may come in a number of different guises. It may, for example, be possible to offer some control to learners over the sequence in which certain topics are studied. More significantly for the development of independent learning, there should be planned opportunities for the individual to decide how she will study. Such occasions should never become a soft option or be seen as an abdication of responsibility by the teacher. Offering choice should always be a way of challenging the individual to a deeper understanding of themselves in general and learning in particular.

- **display self-reliance in finding and using resources**

The growth of electronic means of storing and retrieving information is expanding the opportunities for learning. The independent learner will be aware of the potential of information and communication technology, but also recognise the value of human and textual resources. He will display the capacity to discriminate between resources, synthesise them where necessary, exercise informed choice and recognise where one is more appropriate than another.

- **understand that learning operates at the deep level (intrinsic motivation) as well as the surface level (extrinsic motivation)**

When asked why they attend school, most learners would respond by saying something like *'to learn things'*, or perhaps after further reflection, *'to pass exams'* or *'to get a job'*. These are the instrumental reasons for learning.

They reflect surface attitudes to learning discussed in Section One. The deep approach, through which a learner might find out how an idea or new understanding could change his life, is closer to the intrinsic aims of learning. The independent learner goes beyond facts and skills, to understanding and a realisation of how learning can help him to develop and change as a person.

- **be self-consciously aware of the process of learning, with a capacity to adjust, correct and improve as appropriate**

This is a sophisticated skill, but it lies at the heart of independent learning. It may be actualised only after a lengthy period of experimentation and reflection. The key word here is 'conscious': the learner must be aware of the processes of learning in the first place to be able to make adjustments. That awareness must be focused on effectiveness. Where there is a perceived lack of effectiveness, the independent learner should have the capacity to switch to another approach. This is why this book places emphasis on making learning 'visible'. The teacher can encourage the risk-taking that may lead to mistakes, and then demonstrate how to grow from there.

> Instead of turning away in denial when you make a mistake, you should become a connoisseur of your own mistakes, turning them over in your mind as if they were works of art, which in a way, they are.

Daniel C. Dennett in 'How To Make Mistakes', from *How Things Are*, edited by Brockman and Matson (Weidenfeld and Nicholson, 1995)

- **understand that the learner has personal responsibility for learning, and display the capacity to adapt to prevailing conditions**

Frequently, the conditions under which people are asked to learn are far from ideal: specialist books may be in demand, equipment may break down or computers may be fully booked. In such circumstances, the independent learner will find ways around the problem and not simply give up, blaming poor resources for failure. This kind of resourcefulness is another quality that is key to the development of the independent learner.

- **recognise the value of working in teams**

  Some gifted learners find it frustrating to work in groups. However, it is important to balance the individualism implied by 'independence' with an understanding of the value of working with, and through, others. Very few human activities rely entirely on a single individual for their completion, vital as an individual may be in making things happen.

As teachers encourage learners to develop these skills, they could point to the generally accepted view that, in the future, people will need to train and re-train a number of times in the course of a career. In addition, surveys of employers confirm that flexibility is a highly desired quality, and that careers demanding independent learning skills (media, information technology, the arts) are highly prized by school leavers.

WHAT CAN TEACHERS DO?

To promote independent learning, teachers can:

1 make selective use of anecdotes to relate facts, ideas and principles to the world outside the classroom

2 formulate aims and objectives that include, but go beyond, notions of passing exams and getting jobs and make sure that they are communicated explicitly to learners

3 provide a varied learning diet that balances individual, group and whole-class work

4 encourage a reflective attitude to making mistakes (including your own), which promotes complementary growth

5 make it clear that taking risks with ideas, putting forward an unusual point of view and experimenting is acceptable in your classroom

6 after careful planning, and without abdicating responsibility, offer a variety of possible approaches to a task and allow the learners to choose a route for themselves

7 encourage resourcefulness by discussing varied opportunities for learning (for example, talk to the group about where learning could happen – from television, radio, other people, and not just from resources in school or college)

8 encourage learners to set their own self-test reviews at the end of a topic.

Classroom rewards and recognition

Of course, teachers do not always have to offer rewards in order to have a positive effect on learners. They can recognise success in many different ways. In class, a look, a nod and smile of recognition as a learner answers with particular accuracy or insight can be highly effective. An appropriate comment on written work may be just as powerful as giving a merit mark. Such moments provide recognition of learning success and their effect is cumulative.

Most schools have public mechanisms that veer more towards rewarding positive learner behaviour. The main strategies used by schools to recognise ongoing success are various kinds of merit systems. These may be related to a house or tutor group scheme and carry some pay-off, such as an early release from school at the end of term for consistent attendance.

Presentation evenings for learners who have gained passes at GCSE, A level or GNVQ are a kind of terminal reward and recognition. These events are usually quite well attended since schools have put considerable effort into converting this traditional celebration into an occasion that feels more relevant to young people at the beginning of the new century.

WHAT CAN TEACHERS DO?

1 Determine whether individual learners would prefer public or private congratulations and then act on this insight.

2 Use the success of your best learners beyond school to inspire the efforts of others still in the classroom. To do this successfully you will need to have a system for tracking individuals once they have completed their school careers.

3 Use 'exit counselling' to ensure that you know where learners are going once they leave your school. Give a stamped addressed postcard to everyone who leaves and ask them to return it to you after they have been at university, college or work for four weeks. The postcard should have prompts to identify who the respondent is, where they are and how they are doing.

4 Use any contacts you may have to identify good practice in other organisations. Cast the net widely, and look for ideas that offer support to individuals. Try to come up with ten suggestions under the headings of 'rewards' and 'recognition'. Below are some ideas you might consider.

   ● Write letters of congratulations yourself to learners that you feel have done particularly well, but for outstanding achievement, deliver a letter personally signed by the headteacher.

   ● Set explicit, visible objectives for every lesson; use them as a review device at the end of the lesson.

   ● Remember to praise and criticise performance in detail, not just in general terms.

   ● Build a culture of recognition by commenting positively on the good work that you see other teachers doing.

   ● Institute a 'learner of the month' programme – encourage learners to evaluate their own progress regularly (see Section Ten, page 151).

Using exhibitions to recognise success

Teachers appear to vary considerably in their commitment to a rich learning environment. A tour round any school will reveal many classrooms with vibrant wall displays, but others that have little or nothing in the way of learners' work exhibited. This is unfortunate, since displays of learners' work mirror their achievements and success. However, there are other ways in which a school can use visual material.

Most schools can rely on their art departments to mount exceptional wall displays. Their principle purpose is, of course, to give a recognition to the talents of the students and to stimulate the interest of others such as parents and visitors. However, given the enormous effort put in to mounting such displays, it seems wasteful that their potential is not more fully exploited.

Businesses frequently promote themselves through trade fairs, which draw their name to the attention of the public and customers. They use professionally developed displays that are mounted on boards and assembled anew for a variety of events. The time and energy invested by companies is repaid in terms of increased business.

For a small investment in display stands, schools could create similar kinds of permanent exhibitions that portray the talents and achievements of learners. Indeed, many schools will already have appropriate experience of exhibitions if they hold an annual careers convention, or even just regular open evenings. This experience can be exploited and deployed more widely.

Initially, the display boards could be located in the reception area of the school, and responsibility for producing exhibitions could be rotated around departments, illustrating the variety and depth of the work they do. The aim for a complete academic year could be to mount displays of the full range of work done in the organisation. A non-exhaustive list of interest groups would obviously include all the departments, but there might also be contributions from the Parent Teacher Association, those responsible for catering, extra-curricular clubs and the participants of educational visits, for example. A visually literate member of staff might be prepared to act as a consultant to those who felt lacking in confidence about their own ability to mount a display.

The display boards, once purchased, would be available throughout the year for a variety of purposes. Once one display has had a few weeks of exposure, it should be removed and replaced with something new. However, particularly successful displays could have an extended life through agreements with local businesses to place them in their shop windows, for example. This would maximise the investment in time and effort and build relationships with local companies.

Naturally, companies that need all their window space to display their own goods would not be interested, but those organisations that have space, but no natural products to display – such as banks and building societies – might welcome an opportunity to demonstrate their commitment to the local community. As long as the work is of high quality and reflects well on the host organisation, many businesses would be happy to accommodate a school or college enterprising enough to approach the right person in the right way. Many such organisations have prominent high street locations and could well attract excellent publicity for your craft or science department, for example, particularly if there is a working model to put on show. If you are interested in this idea, start at the local, rather than the regional or national, level.

Stop and think: How much recognition? How much reward?

Think back over your last teaching week. How often did you offer recognition to learners' achievements? What were the circumstances? When were you able to offer a tangible reward? When were your wall displays last changed?

If your memory is not up to recalling incidents from last week, use this topic to audit your practice (see Section Ten).

Comment

You probably found that you offered recognition far more often than reward. This is because meaningful reward is quite difficult for schools. Most of the rewards offered in the outside world – status, money, prestige, promotion – are just not accessible to the teacher. Teachers need to be exceptionally creative in finding meaningful rewards for learners' efforts.

Using public relations and marketing to recognise success

Schools have become increasingly aware of the need for effective marketing strategies. This may be the result of a decision to counter an undeserved negative image in the local community, or to attract new learners to offset falling rolls. However, schools, or indeed individual teachers, rarely recognise the huge potential for improving learner self-image and morale that can come with media exposure.

Seeing their achievements reported in the media has the extraordinary effect of validating learners' accomplishments. This in turn helps learners to build confidence in themselves and in the quality of the school they attend. With the growth in confidence, they become ambassadors whose continued support provides powerful word-of-mouth recommendation for the school. However, the beneficial effects of using the media only come about with a systematic approach to marketing.

Some marketing strategies proceed on the assumption that any publicity is good. The agents of pop stars or actors frequently arrange a photo opportunity that will develop a 'bad boy' or 'bad girl' image. This can never be appropriate for schools and colleges, where the image presented should *always* be positive.

The internal clientele of the school or college should be the principal beneficiaries from effective marketing. A positive image can improve confidence, develop self-awareness and enhance their job prospects. The confidence of all learners, not just those who are featured, will be promoted by seeing or hearing their activities reported in a newspaper, on the radio or on television. Such exposure has automatic prestige and has the effect of verifying individual or school success. Entering into a dialogue with the media can secure a powerful ally for changing perceptions and celebrating success.

The first step for anyone wanting to use the media to recognise the success of learners is to identify the audiences. The subsequent 'marketing' can then be targeted appropriately. Schools lack the sharpness of focus of commercial enterprises when it comes to marketing, so they have to adopt a strategy that can reach out to a much wider audience, consisting of several sectors as described below.

Sector 1: Parents

Parents occupy an unusual position with regard to schools: they are customers as well as suppliers. While parents may be uniquely privileged in this sense, celebrating the success of learners to this sector is a key feature when using the media.

Sector 2: Employers

For Secondary schools, local employers are one of the most obvious 'markets' for their leavers since they will be taking your 'product' next. They will have a number of attitudes and preconceptions that may be favourable or unfavourable to your learners. Astute marketing can challenge an undeserved reputation for poor attendance, unruly behaviour, and so on, and enhance a reputation in the eyes of local employers. Employers may be seen as a specialised group within the community as a whole.

Sector 3: The governors

Most information about a school will come to governors through formal meetings and reports. However, they will also read the local newspaper and hear what people are saying in the community. Therefore, governors too can be influenced by what they see and hear in the media.

Sector 4: The local community

Every educational institution has its neighbours. Their view may be coloured by their own children's experiences of the school, or by memories of someone in a school uniform cutting across their front garden or spraying a rude message on their garage door. Such partial, negative experiences need to be countered by a consistent flow of positive stories of achievement and success. If a school regularly appears towards the bottom of local league tables, the annual exposure of results in the local paper can be off-set by a regular drip-feed of positive stories in other areas of academic activity throughout the year.

You may want to differentiate the local community in a number of ways and consider how you can reach them. For example, there will be parents with children still in the system. They can be reached through a parents' newsletter. Those with no formal connection – for example, those with children in the Primary sector soon to move on to Secondary schools – will probably read a local newspaper or listen to local radio. In the interests of promoting a positive picture of education generally, both groups should be addressed.

Sector 5: The local authority and other educational professionals

Despite the decline of local authority influence, this audience may be a target that is worth influencing through the media. There are, of course, many ways of informing fellow professionals about the positive achievements of a school or college, but the reasons for using newspapers, radio and television are just as valid for this group as for any other.

Stop and think: What are the key audience sectors for you?
Once you have a clear idea of your audience, you can tailor your public relations accordingly. Who are the key people you are trying to reach?

Remember that your own learners may be strongly influenced by seeing themselves in the media. Does the promotion of their self-esteem figure significantly in your planning?

Is this something you can do as an individual or do you think it requires a whole-school approach? How can you begin to influence your school to take a more active approach to recognising learner achievements in this way?

Comment
The most effective marketing strategy will not compensate for a poor 'product'. The recognition or marketing of learner success must be based on strength, success and genuine achievement, otherwise it becomes mere propaganda. Hollow claims will rapidly be exposed and the reputation of the school or college will be diminished as a result.

'Safety–danger' continuum

Once you have identified the audience sectors, the next step is to adopt some method of placing in the local media stories that reflect the activities of all learners. One possible technique is to use the 'safety–danger' continuum. This is a device that can help teachers to monitor stories to reflect the full range of learner activities. At the 'safe' end of the continuum lie stories that reflect solid academic achievement; at the other end are stories that reflect more trivial activities, which nevertheless reflect positive images of learners.

The distinction between 'safe' and 'dangerous' stories is not as clear-cut as it may appear at first sight. There is in fact a continuum running between the two, which can be exploited to give a more balanced view of the range of activities undertaken by your learners. The continuum may be represented as follows.

Safety				Danger
Academic	Pastoral	Visits	Social and Fun	Frivolities

A more detailed commentary on each aspect is given over the page.

Academic

Any story that reflects academic success will attract a positive response from all stakeholders in your organisation.

A party of students investigate the functions of the town Mayor and shadow him or her for a day. Their brief is to look at how the role of the Mayor may change with the introduction of direct elections to the office. Photographs are taken in the Mayor's chambers. The students write up their experiences under the title of *'Lord Mayor for a day'* and their work is heavily quoted in the press report.

Despite indifferent examination results overall, a school has the student with the best GCSE grades in the town. A photograph of the individual holding the results certificate appears in the local press along with an interview revealing *'The secret of my success'*.

Pastoral

Most people recognise that schools should be more than just places for achieving examination success. They are expected to contribute to personal development as well.

A tutor group decides that they are going to hold a Christmas party for children from a nearby school for the disabled. Each student takes responsibility for entertaining one disabled child and agrees to help raise money to finance the party. One enterprising student approaches a local manufacturer of potato crisps and receives a box, free of charge. A story appears under the title *'Local industry helps Christmas cheer'*. (Note that in this story everyone receives some recognition for their contribution; this is a 'win–win' story.)

Visits

This is an easy one for most institutions to exploit.

In any academic year, almost as a matter of routine, there will be a number of visits arranged that can be used to demonstrate the wide range of learning opportunities offered in the school (for example, *'Local school is Domeward bound'*). A photograph of the party about to leave may appear in the local press.

Social and 'fun'

We now move into more contentious areas.

Social activities are recognised by most teachers as having valuable educational outcomes. However, many members of the public, and indeed some staff, view them as distractions from the real business of learning. Nevertheless, many social activities may be regarded as 'safe'. The example below may be considered safe, while a lunchtime disco should be approached with caution.

> A chess club holds a tournament that is won by the youngest entrant ('*Budding grandmaster defeats all-comers*'). A picture features a room full of heads concentrating on the boards.

Schools and colleges need to have some experience of public relations and a good rapport with local journalists before trying to exploit 'fun' events (for example, '*Young designers revise school uniform*'). There may also be some opposition from staff for this type of story – you may encounter the view that school is not about having fun(!) However, as long as it is clear that the event is happening outside normal working hours, there should be no undue cause for concern.

Frivolities

As long as there is confidence that it can balanced by stories of a more serious nature, there is no reason why a school should not release 'frivolous' material (for example, '*Joanne wins long-finger-nail competition*'). The media are in fact quite hungry for such stories and their readers are interested in items that offer a variation from the usual newspaper stories of violence and disaster. The best way to avoid criticism from other staff is to involve them in the planning of the strategy and make the reasons for running stories at the 'danger' end of the continuum absolutely explicit.

Generally, local newspapers and radio will be interested in young people doing things. Newspapers in particular will send a photographer and/or a reporter if a story has a visual impact. At particular times of the year they may have a surplus of certain kinds of story. For example, you could not guarantee placing an item about a carol concert at Christmas time, though they might just select your school to be featured this year if a famous old student or a local celebrity was reading the lesson.

Stop and think: How could the 'safety–danger' continuum apply to you and your determination to recognise learner success?
Spend a few moments reflecting on the 'safety–danger' continuum. Try to supply one story for each of the 'categories' within it. How many do you think you could actually place in your local press? Would it be acceptable in your school to report stories from the 'frivolous' end of the continuum?

Comment
There can be no single approach to recognising learner success through marketing that will meet the requirements of every school. One organisation may decide that appearing once per term in the local newspaper is all that they need to maintain their profile. Another may decide that only stories from the 'safety' end of the continuum are acceptable. Yet another may have a serious need to change perception in a local community and want to use public relations as part of an overall strategy.

Frequency strategy

Complementing the notion of the 'safety–danger' continuum is the 'frequency strategy', which may help to define some targets for those wishing to commit themselves to more serious marketing. The frequency strategy sets out to identify a wider audience for PR activities and sets targets for where and when stories should be placed (Table 9.1).

Table 9.1 Schedule of PR activities

Time period	Medium	Audience
weekly	local press	local
monthly	local radio regional press	regional
termly	regional TV	regional
yearly	press, TV	national

Notice how the local audience folds into the regional, and then the regional into the national one.

The targets implied here are not unattainable. As expertise develops, so will a feel for the kinds of stories that will only run locally, and those that will attract regional or national interest. The use of a frequency strategy should also help to prevent a log-jam of items at any level.

The involvement of young people in media events

Successful relations with the media can lead to a situation where the roles begin to reverse. Instead of a school seeking publicity through press releases, the media may begin to approach you for stories or for contributions to features. Naturally, a media-conscious organisation will try to accommodate these requests, even taking considerable trouble to do so. However, there are dangers.

Any reputable journalist researching a subject such as the drug-taking habits of young people, for example, will avoid mentioning a school by name (*'Young people speak out on drugs'*), but the public of most towns and cities are usually quite capable of identifying the institutions by the locations described or from a school uniform in a photograph. Stories like this do *not* fall into the category of recognising learner success. Their only justification may be to help with the building of good relations with a journalist who is desperate for copy.

A more positive outcome may result from a request to do a feature on some aspect of school. It seems that some stories (*'School meals go haute cuisine'*) remain perennial favourites. Perhaps the police may request help with a road safety video, or a famous former student may prompt a *'What was she like at school?'* feature. However, requests for help with features like this are only made if you have worked to build good, co-operative relationships already.

If you become very good at this, don't be surprised to receive requests from journalists anxiously enquiring whether you have any good stories coming along at the moment: you can bet that they have a problem finding copy!

Stop and think: Where do you go from here?
This Section contains hints and tips that help to reward and recognise learner success. Read through the material again and identify which parts of it have immediate application for you, which you should be considering over the next year, and then those ideas that can only be considered in the long term.

SUMMARY

◆ LEARNER AUTONOMY CAN BE DEFINED UNDER SIX HEADINGS (PAGES 128–30).

◆ THERE ARE ROUTES TO RECOGNISING SUCCESS BOTH WITHIN AND OUTSIDE THE CLASSROOM.

Section Ten

A new beginning

In *Section Ten* we learn that:

- The experiences of one group of learners is the basis for planning for the future, using a classroom audit.

- Teachers are the people best placed to conduct an evaluation of their own work.

- A classroom audit is a methodical approach to reviewing classroom performance.

BACKGROUND

This stage fuses two steps of the Hero's Journey: 'the road back' and 'the resurrection'. While 'the road back' normally appears after 'the reward', 'the resurrection' may occur at any stage of the narrative.

Having faced the 'supreme ordeal' and seized the reward, the hero is now faced with the problem of returning to the 'ordinary world'. This is not always an easy or triumphant passage since heroes are changed by the journey, and the reality they expect to return to may not be as it was before. The known and loved houses and streets of the city, the faithful friends and the old rituals may have lost their charm in the hero's newly educated eyes. The hero may also face jealousy and resentment from those who remained behind.

The return journey itself may present new problems. The forces that appeared to be defeated often regroup and present new challenges to the hero. The threat may be actual as the enemy gathers new strength after being taken by surprise, or the result of the hero's mental anguish and self-doubt. Having overcome apparently impossible odds in the arena, Maximus in *Gladiator* is faced with Commodus' treachery and intrigue, domains in which his control is far less secure. After his victory at Agincourt, Henry's road back also involves intrigue, but in this case the outcome is the diplomatic triumph of his marriage to Katharine (*Henry V*).

The world's literature is full of stories of heroes who have near-death experiences, or survive death itself to bring back messages or teach lessons. The resurrection of Perdita in *The Winter's Tale* is spectacularly trumped by that of Hermione who, reportedly dead for twenty years, suddenly steps down from a plinth where she is represented as a statue to greet her jealous husband and reconcile him with Polixenes. In Shakespeare's most famous romantic tragedy, on the other hand, Romeo and Juliet's only physical resurrection is as statues. Their fate is to act as object lessons in the repercussions of hatred and jealousy between rivals.

APPLICATION

For an adult learner returning to work after a training course, or an unemployed individual using newly acquired qualifications as a route back into work, the lessons of this step of the journey are clear enough. The employee who acquires new skills on a training course must find a way of integrating them into the ordinary world of work, which may be hostile to any innovation brought in from outside. For the unemployed adult travelling the road back into work after a retraining programme, the tests include job applications and interviews followed by a 'resurrection' as an employed person.

The picture for learners in school is not as straightforward. After the reward of GCSE, A level or GNVQ, learners may feel a need to reconsider their new place in the world and make adjustments, but it is more difficult to formalise this self-review into an explicit developmental phase. The picture is further confused because learners in school may be said to take a 'road back' every day as they return home to their ordinary world. The majority will encounter support and help at home, with every step of the journey, but others will have to struggle to continue their quest in the face of heavy odds (see also Section Seven, page 100).

The remainder of this Section continues the analysis of the feelings and reactions of learners at this stage of the journey. However, the focus shifts even more emphatically onto the actions of the teacher. This is because the learner has begun to move beyond the teacher at this stage, and there is less direct influence to be exerted. In a sense, the teacher/mentor's journey takes precedence and the lessons learned in working with the older generation of learners become the raw material for inspiring the new. This step could be defined as a time of further reflection, which animates a new beginning.

How can teachers focus that new beginning? One answer may be to use a more systematic approach to review and development. All teachers instinctively know when something has gone well and informally incorporate the lessons learned into their future teaching. This is part of the art of teaching. This Section considers how to add systematic analysis to intuition in the interest of improving classroom practice.

Classroom audit

A classroom audit may be defined as the systematic analysis of the quality of teaching, including:

- the techniques used for developing the knowledge, skills and understanding students need
- the use of resources and the resulting outcomes in terms of learner understanding
- learner independence
- examination success.

This may seem a long and involved definition, but basically audit is a process of review and improvement of what happens in classrooms. The process has been given the title of 'classroom audit', but the simple techniques involved can also be applied to reviewing the structures, processes and outcomes of a school as a whole.

Some characteristics of a classroom audit

The audit process is based on the use of standards to promote quality in teaching and learning. The use of standards in the classroom, in common with their use in general, is designed to:

- stimulate discussion (*'What are we doing that is good? What needs changing?'*)
- promote good practice (*'Are we doing as well as we should be?'*)
- reduce misunderstanding (*'Are we sure that everyone involved is clear about who, what, when, why and how?'*)
- inspire change (*'Where next?'*).

The audit should take the minimum amount of effort on the part of the teacher, generate the maximum amount of benefit and should never divert attention from the learning process itself. The audit should also:

- be short-term in its period of application, but long-term in its effects
- be a systematic approach, which identifies opportunities for improvements and provides a mechanism for bringing them about
- never involve risk to the learners' progress
- never involve disturbance to normal classroom management.

The role of the teacher in conducting an audit

The use of standards in promoting learning in classrooms is becoming increasingly common. In England and Wales, the performance threshold assessment standards for classroom teachers have brought their use sharply into focus but many teachers will already have been aware of them through the Teacher Training Agency Standards for headteachers, heads of department and classroom teachers. An audit takes advantage of the opportunity afforded by the wider availability of standards and demonstrates how to make them viable for use in the classroom.

As a professional who interacts with his group of students on a regular basis, the teacher is the individual best placed to determine which standards should be applied to his teaching. It is also the teacher who is best placed to examine practice and make improvements in the light of observations. However, there is a place for a neutral observer who can provide objective comment on aspects of classroom management. In addition, school managers may want to have some influence over how a teacher's efforts are deployed. But the role of the manager or the outsider can only be a marginal one compared with that of the teacher, whose instincts are formed by daily contact with individuals and groups.

It is the teacher's role to determine which aspects of classroom practice should be audited. It may be necessary to consult with school managers regarding whole-school priorities, but the individual teacher knows where his strengths and weaknesses lie. Once that is agreed, the next step is to identify relevant external standards or produce internal ones, identify the criteria and decide on a methodology for monitoring performance.

The process may be represented as a cyclical model, as shown below.

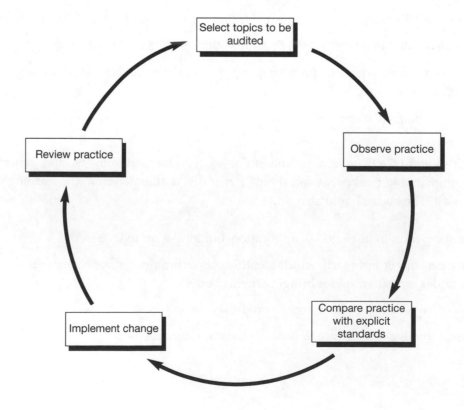

Note that unless 'implement change' actually happens, the process is valueless to learners. Even if the teacher finds that practice is good, ways should still be found of making it even better.

Teachers are strongly recommended to discuss any ideas for a classroom audit with a curriculum manager, or any individual who can credibly act in a mentoring role, and use her as a reference point. Working alone may be more expedient in the short term, but it can also be frustrating and demoralising.

Developing standards and criteria

Standards attempt to state explicitly how learning should be managed. They represent a notion of the 'right' way of delivering learning. There are also implicit standards, which are more a question of tone and which many teachers will have absorbed without really questioning how they came to be incorporated into their professional persona. Implicit standards may, for example, form part of a belief system about the need for kindliness, courtesy and respect for human dignity when dealing with learners. These qualities are really a function of personality and as such are not amenable to the audit process.

Standards are at the core of the audit process. However, on their own they lack the precision needed to be useful in analysing classroom practice. Therefore, the next step after identifying or defining standards is to derive some **criteria**. These are definable and measurable items that describe quality and can be used to assess it.

For example, one criterion drawn from the key skill in communication 'Take part in discussions', is:

> (Learners) must make contributions, which are relevant to the subject and purpose.

This only becomes measurable when criteria are added:

> **All** learners **(100%)** must make contributions, **on at least three distinct occasions in a term,** which are relevant to the subject and purpose.

Although this does not address one key part of the standard (*'relevant to the subject and purpose'*), which can only be decided in individual circumstances, the added criteria do make it possible for the learner to achieve the standard because they provide a way for the teacher to measure the learner's oral contributions. In other words, adding criteria here helps with the quantity, but not the quality, of the contribution.

The example given above identifies one standard and adds two criteria to help teachers measure quantity in learner contributions. However, standards and criteria are unlikely to exist in isolation like this. Taken together, they can be used to build up a 'map' of best practice. Nevertheless, in the early stages of implementing a classroom audit, it may be wise to work through one standard at a time until sufficient expertise develops.

Stop and think: Adding criteria
Take any standard from a published source and consider how it can be refined using appropriate criteria. Which standards set out below (adapted from the key skill 'Working with others', Level 2) do you think can be refined by the addition of criteria? Assume that you want to audit the competence of a whole class, rather than an individual learner.

Learners must:
- follow working methods accurately
- organise own activities so as to meet own responsibilities efficiently and effectively
- bring difficulties affecting their ability to meet own responsibilities, promptly to the attention of the teacher
- give feedback on progress of own work, which is clear and based on appropriate evidence.

Comment
It is tempting to add criteria like '100% of the learners, 100% of the time' to these standards, but that is hardly feasible. The challenge is to define criteria that reflect a lively engagement with learning. For example, the third standard in the list, 'bring difficulties affecting the ability to meet own responsibilities, promptly to the attention of the teacher' implies the questions 'How often would you expect learners to ask for further help?' *and* 'How successful are you as a teacher in encouraging learners to ask for help in clarifying working instructions?' *This might lead to the addition of criteria like* '**Over the course of a term, 75% of learners** should bring difficulties affecting their ability to meet own responsibilities, promptly to the attention of the teacher **on at least one occasion.**'

These criteria should be discussed with other teachers who may have higher or lower expectations. From such discussions, a consensus may begin to emerge about how successful your school is in promoting co-operative working.

Internal and external standards

Standards may be acquired from external sources, or developed internally. External standards may come from the key skills or those published for the performance threshold assessment or by the Teacher Training Agency.

Internal standards may be developed by a school, or indeed an individual teacher. However, care should be exercised with internal standards since they may be too parochial and fail to reflect best practice. This 'bench marking' aspect is important in determining standards. Wherever possible, the levels of achievement should be determined using comparable schools that are recognised as being highly successful. This means that like should be compared with like.

The availability of objective, comparable measures of performance is one advantageous result of externally set standards. School league tables are a useful source of this kind of information. However unpopular they may be with teachers, the league tables have drawn attention to what the best schools are doing in terms of examination results and the wide variations that exists between those with comparable intakes of students. Before league tables, such measures were not readily accessible.

Another reason for using externally set standards is that internally generated ones are time-consuming to construct. However, those that are produced internally are more likely to arouse a sense of ownership, which helps to foster commitment. This is important in carrying an audit through to a successful conclusion in terms of changing classroom practice (Table 10.1).

Table 10.1 The relative merits of internally and externally set standards

Externally set standards	Internally set standards
constructed from a wide research base	constructed from local experience
supported by a recognised authoritative body	local feeling of 'ownership' builds motivation and a stronger commitment to implement results
established	adaptable to local circumstances
no effort in construction	time-consuming to construct

A sensible compromise would be to combine internally and externally set standards in constructing the 'map' of quality that was mentioned earlier (page 145). For example, most externally set standards will lack the criteria needed to make them relevant to a specific classroom situation. Adding the criteria is the most powerful way of customising external standards to local needs.

Standards are not necessarily fixed, but may be adapted to local circumstances. These adaptations are the 'allowable exceptions' that occur in most audit projects. Allowable exceptions are those cases that should be excluded from the study because their presence would distort the findings. For example, a group with a large number of students whose first language is not English might distort an audit into the frequency with which discussion takes place, or the extent to which individuals request clarification of instructions. However, care should always be exercised when specifying the allowable exceptions since this may lead to a justification for inferior performance and classifying poor practice as acceptable. In other words, standards may be adapted in such a way that any challenge is diminished, rather than promoting uncomfortable comparisons with the best in the field.

Sources of standards for audit

There are a number of reliable sources for obtaining educational standards. The most obvious ones in the UK are:

- key skills standards (for schools, those at NVQ levels 1 to 3)
- Teacher Training Agency standards (for example, for newly qualified teachers)
- OFSTED standards
- performance threshold assessment standards.

However, classroom teachers may also like to consider other sources such as the six indicators of learning autonomy given in Section Nine (pages 128–30) or the sets of standards at the back of *Classroom Management* by Philip Waterhouse and Chris Dickinson (Network Educational Press, 2001), which offer one hundred indicators for the classroom teacher.

Structure, process and outcome

Standards may be applied to any one of the three characteristic phases of education: structure, process and outcome.

Structural criteria and standards describe the environment for learning. They may refer to the nature of the service provided, the building, staffing and professional development. Typical structural audits might look at internal and external communications, such as how often the school appears in the media (see Section Nine), school–home liaison, parents' evenings, student attendance, participation in extra-curricular activities and use of exhibitions and wall displays.

Process criteria and standards describe the way that learning is managed. There may be considerations of student induction, movement around the school, effectiveness of various teaching techniques and use of the library.

Outcome, naturally enough, describes the effects of teaching and may involve considerations of parent satisfaction, test and examination results, placement of learners in the next stage of education and employers' perceptions of their new recruits.

Choosing a topic for audit

It is important in choosing a topic for audit that it can be:

- expressed in terms of standards

- measured against agreed criteria

- audited within the sample available

- certain of attracting support from a manager or colleague with the necessary expertise to offer guidance in auditing.

The outcomes should:

- lead to improvements in school or classroom practice

- repay the investment of time and effort (and possibly money).

The benefits should be:

- relevant to professional practice

- in line with organisational priorities.

Stop and think: Identifying standards appropriate to you and your work

Devise your own standards or adopt them from published sources to cover some aspect of your work. This aspect could relate to:

- structure – for example, home–school contacts, industry links, timetable construction or cleanliness of the building
- process – for example, the attractiveness and relevance of wall displays, the quality of learning resources, questioning technique or the variety of learning experiences offered
- outcomes – for example, examination results, success in entries to the next phase of education or positive comments from local employers

Try to refine the standards by adding measurable criteria.

Methodology

There are a number of audit methods available for the analysis of quality. However, the one discussed in this Section – criterion-based audit – is the natural complement to the use of standards in measuring classroom performance. It is appropriate to the classroom teacher who wants to measure his practice against bench marks of quality. Groups of teachers may work collaboratively to improve the quality of their work.

The teacher(s) will set the standards and criteria after initial thought and consultation with curriculum managers. This takes some time and effort and it is worthwhile going to some trouble to get it right before beginning analysis. From the start, be sure that you are confident that the standards chosen are:

- defined precisely
- responsive to objective measurement
- appropriate to the topic chosen
- applicable to the individual or team's own practice
- manageable in number (auditing one standard is quite respectable, three may be the maximum that a teacher working alone can handle at one time).

Summary

A checklist that summarises the steps in conducting an audit is given below:

1 **Identify a broad area for audit.** For the classroom teacher this may be:

- aspects of learning design (see Section Twelve, page 169)
- questioning technique (see Section Four, page 67)
- quality of learners' written work and assessment
- homework completion
- levels of learner independence in accessing resources.

2 **Define appropriate standards.** These may be arrived at externally from:

- key skills (NVQ levels 1–3)
- OFSTED
- Teacher Training Agency
- performance threshold assessment
- known centres of excellence
- other published sources.

Alternatively, internal standards can be set through consultation with:

- colleagues
- department managers
- school managers
- colleagues in other institutions
- other sources of expertise (for example, inspectors).

3   **Refine standards with measurable criteria** that are appropriate to local practice. Such criteria should be realistic, but demanding. The purpose of setting criteria is to make comparisons with comparable schools that are recognised as being the best. For example, if you set out to audit students' use of the library, it may be demotivating to set a criterion derived from a single unit school with linked buildings if your school occupies a split site.

4   **Collect the information that you need**. Teachers working in classrooms may need some help in collecting data. However, an audit of questioning technique that has the criterion '*100% learner participation in class question-and-answer sessions over a three week period*' could be audited simply by ticking names in a mark book as learners respond to questioning. Other techniques the classroom teacher can use include:

   ● survey or questionnaire information from learners

   ● survey or questionnaire information from parents, employers and other external sources

   ● results of tests

   ● self-generated video evidence of classroom processes

   ● co-operation with a colleague or curriculum manager.

5   **Discuss the findings** with colleagues, a mentor or manager. One of the benefits of an audit is that it encourages teachers to compare their practice with that of others. This may lead to the discovery that what one teacher considered to be standard practice is in fact outstanding. However, the reverse may also be true.

6   **Implement changes to classroom practice**. Unless this stage is activated then the whole audit process is a waste of time. There must be tangible outcomes to justify the effort expended. The objective of improving school or classroom processes, with concrete outcomes for learners, must be built into audit processes from the beginning.

7   **Monitor the results** to check whether changes have resulted in improvement. Once the change is implemented, the process must make provision for checking that the improvements are sustained. This implies that there may need to be a number of passes through the audit cycle on the same topic after a suitable period of time to allow the changes in technique to bed down.

8   **Identify the next audit topic**.

Evaluating learning

Most teachers will be familiar with post-training evaluation. This has become almost a ritualised attempt to assess the value of a course or programme and the impact of the trainer's performance. The evaluation sheets are distributed and conference delegates or course participants fill them in. The intentions behind such assessments are usually honourable and some trainers do indeed incorporate comments and suggestions from previous sessions into their next event. However, despite most teachers' familiarity with the use of participant evaluation, very few ever use it with learners in the classroom.

The reasons for this are numerous. It may be that teachers do not think that younger learners are in any position to evaluate their learning experiences, or they may simply be afraid of what their classes might have to say. Whatever the reason, it is unfortunate that teachers make so little use of learner evaluation, since this can be an excellent source of information about learner perceptions. At the very least, where misapprehensions are revealed through evaluation, they can be corrected by the teacher.

One way of using evaluation without seeming to invite comments from learners on the quality of teaching or the teacher is to ask them to evaluate the level of their understanding after a lesson or module of work.

Stop and think: Why evaluate learning?
What is the value of using learners to evaluate their own experience?
Spend a few moments considering the value of evaluating learning. What can you learn from evaluation that you could not learn simply from testing?

Comment
Testing will tell us whether learners have absorbed information and the extent to which they have made it a part of their learning landscape. Evaluation offers us additional information such as:

- *how confident learners are about their learning*
- *whether the approach adopted by the teacher suited the material and matched the learners' preferences*
- *what can be done to make improvements.*

Teachers embarking on a classroom audit need to be aware of the potential of questionnaires for distorting outcomes.

The learner's perspective

If the teacher is keen to develop the deep approach to learning, one of the key questions to be asked is '*How has the learning changed the individual?*'

When extracting learners' reactions to a learning experience, you can either concentrate on specifics or rely on a general response. Both have their advantages and disadvantages. If you want to test reactions to a particular aspect of learning, then obviously a reaction sheet that draws attention to these specific issues will be appropriate. On the other hand, a blank sheet of paper and an invitation to record comments can elicit some revealing insights.

Too many reaction sheets allow learners to 'sit on the fence' by offering a three- or five-point scale of reaction. If you want to get a clearer picture of how well the teaching was received, use a four-point scale. This requires learners to opt clearly for a decision that favours either 'satisfactory' or 'unsatisfactory'. However, you may feel that offering an evaluation like this is inappropriate and would prefer to avoid 'marking' in this sense at all.

Set out below is an example of a reaction evaluation sheet that combines a call for detailed response with space for general comment. It avoids the 'personal' element of a class assessing a teacher by concentrating on their perceptions of how much they have learned.

Following our module of work on Statistics, please rate your understanding of:	Good	Satisfactory	Unsatisfactory	Poor
mean				
median				
mode				
…				
We used two different approaches to learning in this module. Which did you prefer?				
Why did you prefer this approach?				

One of the additional benefits of evaluating learning in this way is that individual learners, who may have been reticent in the classroom setting, can admit to deficiencies without embarrassment. However, as with all evaluation, you are dependent on the respondents telling the truth.

While there is more of a place for direct comment from learners than teachers generally allow, there should be at least one other measure of success or failure that offers more objective analysis of how effective learning has been.

Objective information such as testing is not always easy to collect. It takes more planning and effort than subjective comment and as such consumes more of a teacher's most precious resource – time.

SUMMARY

◆ A CLASSROOM AUDIT IS A SYSTEMATIC APPROACH TO ANALYSING CLASSROOM PERFORMANCE.

◆ STANDARDS FORM THE BASIS OF A CLASSROOM AUDIT.

◆ STANDARDS SHOULD BE REFINED BY USING MEASURABLE CRITERIA THAT ARE DEMANDING BUT REALISTIC.

Closure

In Section Eleven we learn that:

- The ordinary world of the learner will be transformed by the learning experience.

- Teachers can help learners to integrate themselves back into the ordinary world.

- Skills such as the ability to cope with change, manage time and maintain their own morale are vital for learners' further growth.

BACKGROUND

This stage parallels the 'return with the elixir' step of the Hero's Journey. It completes the circle of growth and development as the hero finally re-enters the ordinary world. If there has been disruption to that world, then order is restored.

In both *Ulysses* and *The Lord of the Rings*, the heroes have to cleanse their ordinary worlds of the undesirable gangs that have moved in as occupying forces. For some heroes, it appears that there is no rest from the demands of the journey. In both cases, the cleansing is accomplished with ease. Nevertheless, the homecoming is not what they had expected or hoped for. This bitter–sweetness is a common theme in Hero's Journey stories. It serves as a dose of reality, which offsets any sentimentality or idealisation of the ordinary world.

Even as Dorothy taps her heels together and intones, *'There's no place like home'* at the end of *The Wizard of Oz*, her new self-awareness means that Kansas is not as she remembered it. Home may be where the heart is, but it is now transformed not only by the relief of her return, but also the magic of greater confidence and poise.

For narratives where the hero has strayed from the path, an external force is required to restore harmony. At the end of each of Shakespeare's tragedies, a character untainted by the previous action (Fortinbras in *Hamlet*, Albany in *King Lear*, Malcolm in *Macbeth* and Lodovico in *Othello*) steps in to re-establish order in the ordinary world after the corruption introduced by the main characters.

APPLICATION

This final stage of the learner's journey is concerned with integrating the learner into the ordinary world using the 'elixirs' she brings with her. These ordinary worlds include further learning in other institutions and work with training attached. Some may end up in dead-end jobs or drawing benefit, but the majority will follow progressive routes that offer opportunity and growth.

Your learners will leave you with many of their attitudes and opinions fully formed. Their point of view will be coloured by their experience of learning with you, by their social and cultural background and by their capacity to adapt and grow. These overlap in complex ways to form an individual personality. These perspectives are explored in more detail below. They are separated here for convenience, not because this arrangement reflects reality.

Many adults believe that learning stops once people leave school. What they fail to recognise is that the absorption of new skills and information is often unconscious. However, there are still some formal demands for learning. For example, the written part of the driving test has stimulated an awareness that the learning techniques picked up at school are not quite as irrelevant as some learners had thought.

Dealing with previous experience

Most people's memories of learning will continue to be dominated by school long after they have left. If you try a word-association exercise with leavers, they will probably respond to the word 'school' with a range of associations. These will be positive for the most part, but for some the connection will be painful. All the good teaching that they received may be offset by a single poor teacher; all the fun that they had will be forgotten because of an incident of bullying or unreasonable punishment.

These sour memories need to be purged. If you have access to learners at the end of their programmes, encourage recall of learning *successes* – wherever they were achieved. Point out that if learning comes easily, we tend to think it was something other than learning that happened. Give examples of things that people learn without even realising it. Ask learners to check if they know:

- the words of pop songs
- the complex arithmetic of snooker (*'With x number of balls on the table, can you beat an opponent's score of y or will snookers be needed?'*) or darts (*'What combination of trebles and doubles do you need for a finish from 87 in three darts?'*)

- the history of their favourite sports team
- the rules of a game
- the multiple storylines of a soap opera.

There may be many other examples of unconscious learning that you could draw on. Much of what people learn at work they seem to have somehow absorbed. The same is true of skills. Encourage learners to reflect on these as learning opportunities and to be prepared to grasp them when they occur in the future.

Refuse to allow anyone to run down their potential for learning, their own accomplishments or those of others. Do not allow anyone to say, *'I am only a ...'*, or *'I couldn't possibly do that, it's too difficult for me ...'*.

Ask learners to look carefully at what they have learned and the skills they have acquired. Try to get them to see how they have done it. Could the same techniques be applied in other situations?

Social and cultural influences

Along with understanding language, social and cultural influences are one of the earliest forms of learning that we encounter. For some people, these early influences remain so powerful that they resist change even when the evidence overwhelmingly suggests that they are untrue. There are many examples of individuals who cling to prejudice and intolerance simply to protect an idiosyncratic version of reality.

The teacher is a transmitter of certain cultural and social values. However, this is rarely, if ever, discussed by teachers, despite sometimes being the cause of considerable antagonism.

One of the first (but unwritten) rules of professional responsibility is to recognise how your own cultural identity shapes your attitudes. While everyone recognises that it is difficult to be entirely objective in every situation, we should all be on our guard against assuming that 'boys will be engineers' and 'girls will be hairdressers'. We should be particularly careful when our experience appears to confirm the reality of a stereotype. To a large extent learners will want to conform and 'fit in' with prevailing norms of behaviour and expectations. Through their expectations, teachers are in a position to exert considerable influence on learners. It is therefore a professional responsibility to exercise care about what those expectations are.

Coping with change

Most organisations, both public and private, have undergone rapid and fundamental change in recent years. Traditional jobs have disappeared at an alarming rate. We have had 'privatisations', 'downsizing', 'de-layering', 'competitive tendering' and a number of other changes that have made employment less secure. Adjusting to the new realities has been painful for many people.

It is easy to feel dispirited and dehumanised in the face of the powerful forces affecting our lives, but our job as teachers is to prepare learners for what they will encounter in the outside world. Change may be frightening, but it always means new opportunities as well as imminent threats. For many people, the job in which they are working now may not have existed ten or even five years ago. The new approaches to work have brought benefits and fulfilment as well as anxiety.

Stop and think: How have you dealt with change?
What changes have occurred in your adult and working life over the last five years? What changes occurred in your adult and working life over the five years prior to that? In which of these two periods did most change occur?

What changes do you expect to see over the next five years? What changes do you expect to occur in your adult and working life by 2050?

Comment
The conclusions you may have drawn from this activity are that:
- *society is changing*
- *the pace of change is speeding up*
- *change itself is changing*
- *it is becoming more and more difficult to predict the future.*

If teaching is to have any value it must prepare people for an adult and working life that is becoming increasingly unpredictable. What knowledge, skills and understanding will people need?

Stop and think: What are your predictions for the future?
Look at the following predictions of what a young person leaving school can expect to experience during his lifetime. Ask yourself, 'To what extent has this happened to me?'

Most people can expect:
- at least two major changes of career
- a wide variety of working patterns, involving different types of jobs and changes in employer
- to move away from the area in which they were born
- re-training throughout their lives
- one or more periods of unemployment
- two or three long-term relationships.

Comment
These predictions were first made in 1979 so we can expect some of them to have already come true and to have become more extreme. They raise a number of questions.

What knowledge, skills and understanding are required in order to cope with these possible experiences? What changes in our teaching methods are needed?

A partial answer to these questions has already been suggested in Section Nine, where the value of independent learning is considered (page 128), but what other instruments do today's learners need in their tool bag to cope with their future lives and work?

Adventures in Learning

Managing morale

Career paths have changed dramatically in the last 20 years. Jobs for life have virtually disappeared and an increasing number of people work on short-term contracts. There is intensifying uncertainty about the future and a sometimes painful sense of betrayal because an organisation in which an individual has invested a lifetime of devotion and effort suddenly turns round and asks for something more, or something different, or, most painful of all, that the person should leave.

Today, staying in work, in any kind of interesting or challenging job, means continuing to learn. Either individuals take responsibility for their own personal and professional development or they end up without the skills and knowledge needed to carry a career forwards.

Sometimes the speed of change can be too rapid. Confidence may take a knock and in this kind of atmosphere it is perhaps only natural that people should look for someone to blame. Somehow or other, 'they' should do something about what is going on. Blaming others like this is a pointless exercise since often those perceived to be responsible are themselves subject to the same forces of change. These attitudes are often picked up by learners in schools and reflected in a willingness to blame others for personal shortcomings.

One of the consequences of the change in the relationship between employers and employees – between managers and the managed – is that responsibility for morale, how people feel about themselves, has been shifted to the shoulders of the individual. The reason is simple – in industry there are fewer managers around now to worry about how people are feeling.

We all recognise that a learner's confidence may be affected if one of his best ideas is dismissed as worthless, or he is criticised for something that he could not control, or all the work he does on a project is wasted because someone else does not do their part. In situations like this it is up to the teacher to encourage learners to display the resilience to bounce back and re-establish their self-confidence. If learners allow negative feelings to dominate, their self-respect will nose-dive.

Stop and think: How do you cope with negativity?
If something negative does happen to you in the course of your work, how do you deal with it? How can you encourage learners to apply similar tactics?

Comment
It does not really help simply to tell people that everyone goes through bad times and that they should buck up. Nevertheless, there is a greater expectation now that individuals will take more responsibility for their own attitudes and not rely on others to maintain their morale.

However, this is not to assert that criticism is always counter-productive. One of the roles of the mentor is to tell the hero the truth. At their most useful, critical friends like this can identify areas for improvement that might have remained unexplored. Constructive criticism can point the way to improvement.

Another strategy is to share feelings with someone else, but most people prefer to do this only occasionally and in specific circumstances. Alternatively, you could suggest that learners should marshal their personal resources and lift themselves out of those gloomy feelings of disappointment. The first step is to put the situation into perspective – it would be out of proportion to allow one negative experience to outweigh ten that have gone well. However, there is no doubt that negative criticism hurts much more than positive comments delight – it takes at least three positive comments to offset one negative remark.

WHAT CAN TEACHERS DO?

1 Encourage learners to use action plans, however basic they may be. This will act as a valuable introduction to the experience of agreeing training plans, which they can expect to do repeatedly in their future working lives. An action plan represents an agreement to achieve certain outcomes by a specific time. An action plan should set out aims, objectives, targets and milestones. In addition, the plan could specify the resources that will be allocated to the programme and the support that will be offered to help in achieving the agreed goals. An action plan should cover:

   ● the aims of the programme for the specific individual

   ● targets and milestones to be achieved

   ● a broad outline of what is to be done

   ● those responsible for implementing the various aspects of the plan

   ● how and when progress will be reviewed.

2 Most teachers will be familiar with action plans. However, remember that learners will be less well-versed and may need to have a plan explained to them carefully.

3 Help learners to identify learning opportunities wherever they occur by drawing attention to learning that occurs outside school, and the success that many achieve in this realm.

4 Encourage learners to 'add up' their attributes, skills and talents from which they can draw strength when things are not going so well. Encourage learners to include examples from their personal and social life as well as from school work.

5 Encourage positive self-talk by asking learners to answer questions like *'What am I good at?'*, *'Which parts of my life are going well at the moment?'*, *'Who do I know who can help?'*

6 The longer learners dwell on negative events or missed opportunities, the more they will feel pessimistic and gloomy. Train your learners to see the positive. Run a brief project asking them to make a note of the positive things that happen to them in the course of a day. Try to find a set number of items to note in a day – five should not be too many. The events could be mundane and everyday, such as completing a paper round, receiving courteous treatment from a shopkeeper or arriving at school on time. Ten minutes at the beginning of the day exploring the possibilities should produce a far greater number of examples. They could start a notebook for this activity or use a section of their homework diaries.

Presenting a positive image

Encourage learners to understand the importance of always presenting a positive image of themselves. One way in which most schools do this is by insisting on the wearing of a school uniform. Among other functions, and despite frequent subversions, learners recognise what schools are trying to do. This accounts for the continued support for uniforms from parents and the majority of learners in schools.

There are two types of uniform: the ones that we choose for ourselves and the ones someone else chooses for us. Examples of the former may include sports kit or evening wear. We are usually unconcerned about this type of uniform and are happy, even proud, to wear it, perhaps unconscious of the fact that we are wearing a uniform at all. The uniforms that others choose for us include works overalls or formal clothing denoting rank and status, such as the uniforms worn in the armed forces. Teachers from countries where school uniforms are not as common as they are in Britain will invariably point out that their students adopt the 'informal uniform of jeans and T-shirt'.

Employers too may have dress codes of one sort or another. There are a number of reasons why they insist that certain kinds of clothing should be worn. For example, they want their staff to be easily recognised by members of the public or they guarantee a certain minimum standard of smartness. In a sense, school uniforms help to prepare young people for employers' demands.

For some people, work means meeting the public and representing their organisation. For them, presenting themselves positively is an integral part of the job. Perhaps the most obvious example of this type of job is a receptionist or someone working in sales or public relations. At the other extreme, there are those who have no need to consider how they are perceived by others since in the course of their work they hardly ever meet anyone from outside their organisation. Perhaps a technician working in a laboratory or a computer operator might fall into this group. However, even employers in these sectors will often support a dress code as a mark of respect for co-workers.

WHAT CAN TEACHERS DO?

1 *'You only get one chance to make a first impression.'* A cliché perhaps, but do you think it has any validity? Use work-experience to explore the issue of presenting a positive image. You could discuss ten jobs with learners and then ask them to group them along a continuum like this.

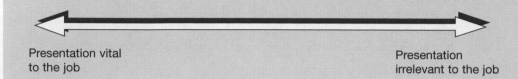

Presentation vital
to the job

Presentation
irrelevant to the job

2 Discuss how important presentation is for a teacher. What is 'the right impression'?

Organising time

Time is a resource. However, unlike other resources, it is inelastic. No matter how high the demand, you cannot make it stretch further to accomplish your aims. By comparison, money is relatively easy to come by and manage. Therefore, we can define time management as the manipulation of a finite resource in order to maximise what can be accomplished and minimise unproductive demands.

One of the more thankless tasks that teachers encounter is educating young people to make better use of their time. After all, for them time appears to be infinite, and there to be wasted indiscriminately. Time management is one of the many skills that teachers try to program into learners, though it is only likely to become active well after they have left school.

When we talk about good time management, we tend to mean:

- getting the maximum done in the time available

- avoiding wastage of time through unnecessary activities

- setting priorities and sticking to them

- having the time to do a job properly and not having to cut corners

- dividing time equitably between our various commitments including personal and professional.

The three steps to good time management are to:

- record time

- consolidate time

- manage time.

Recording time

Any attempt to make better use of time must begin with the way individuals work at the moment. Unfortunately, memory is a very poor indicator of the time we actually allocate to tasks. We tend to think we devote time to those activities we know we *ought* to set as priorities, rather than to the ones we *actually* spend most time on.

Consolidating time

Consolidating time does not just mean working for long periods at a time. It also entails:

- finding out what works for the individual learner
- creating time to use at the individual's discretion
- setting priorities
- minimising interruptions
- finding an appropriate place to work
- scheduling tasks over which you have control to suit your preferred working methods.

Managing time

Managing time is usually a matter of common sense, but sometimes it is the conscious decision not to allow others to break a rhythm. Simple rules like this can help learners of any age to manage their time more efficiently.

Decision making is the key to managing time effectively. Our time is governed by other people's demands and our own habits. Developing good working habits and routines early in life and sticking to them repays the initial effort many times over. Above all, others' priorities should only be allowed to take precedence after careful consideration.

WHAT CAN TEACHERS DO?

1   Decide on one time-saving idea that you are going to use from now on and communicate that idea to your learners. Ask them to come up with at least one idea of their own.

2   Use the simple time log shown overleaf with your learners. The spaces should be used to record blocks of time, daily goals and comments, but the specifics of how you use it are unimportant. Advise learners to use the following method to ensure that the log is useful, relevant and current:

- run the logging activity for 2–3 weeks, twice a year
- record the times when the event is taking place (they should not rely on memory)
- warn learners to include the demands that others make on them at home, in their social commitments and in their academic work
- encourage learners to re-think and re-work their work schedule after each period (see over).

	6–8am	8–10am	10–12noon	12–2pm	2–4pm	4–6pm	6–8pm	8–10pm	...
Week 1									
Monday									
Tuesday									
Wednesday									
Thursday									
Friday									
Saturday									
Sunday									
Week 2									
...									

When they have logged their time for a 2–3 week period, encourage learners to 'prune' their activities accordingly. Remember to run the exercise again in six months time. Show learners how to adjust their programmes depending on current demands:

- advise learners to set aside specific times each week when they do certain tasks, but review their usefulness regularly and ruthlessly

- suggest that learners should involve others in the process, getting them to help in deciding which times are best for work

- point out to learners that they should encourage others to leave them alone at key working periods

- encourage learners to be assertive and to refuse to allow working time to be whittled away

- learners should always set themselves deadlines, but help them to check that they are realistic

- encourage learners to grant themselves small, short-term rewards for achieving targets.

Effective time management is increasingly important in a world that puts so much pressure on individuals to perform consistently.

Understanding organisations

It is important that learners understand how organisations work and how individuals fit into them. The days when people were employed to do only a specific task and information was restricted on a 'need-to-know' basis are long gone. In modern organisations, the reverse is required. Employees are now expected to understand how their work contributes to the organisation as a whole. The Investors in People standard makes specific reference to the need for everyone in the organisation to know and understand its overall aims, objectives and structure.

WHAT CAN TEACHERS DO?

1   Introduce organisational structures by asking learners to draw a diagram with themselves in the centre. Radiating from that central point, they should sketch in all the people with whom they interact directly. Colour codes are useful for discriminating between different contacts and dotted lines can illustrate particular communications pathways (for example, people they speak to personally, or on the telephone).

2   Use an institution that learners know and understand – the school – as an introduction to understanding organisations. Ask learners to draw up a simple chart showing who occupies what position.

3   The hierarchical method of showing an organisation is called an 'organogram'. Sometimes they are turned upside down so that the 'manager' appears at the bottom, suggesting that her major function is to support the work of others.

4   Require learners to draw up similar organisational charts as part of their work-experience.

Encourage learners to be opportunists

Changing work patterns mean that employees now are expected to be problem solvers. This applies not only to the problems that are encountered directly as part of a working responsibility, but also those that occur peripherally. These are the issues where we would perhaps like to turn a blind eye, hoping that someone else will sort it out. The temptation is to avoid such problems if they do not directly impinge on one's own work.

The growth in the need for problem solving is partly the result of changes in organisations and working patterns. Change inevitably brings with it a need to make new adjustments to people and circumstances. In order to cope with these, what is needed are people who can take care of problems, not just point them out. There are plenty of people around who are willing to pass responsibility on to others, complaining that management does not take care of these things as they should. We're all experts at passing the blame, dodging personal responsibility and criticising others.

New working practices require people who have the capacity to spot opportunities for improvement and act on them. This goes beyond immediate work and perhaps even beyond immediate roles.

If we encourage learners to point the finger at others less, and assume ownership of problems more, then job satisfaction improves and career prospects are enhanced. This is what the word 'opportunist' means in this context: enlightened self-interest leading to improved performance.

Organisational policies

Working in a modern organisation means understanding and acting on organisational policies. There is a legal requirement that employers must publish policies for health and safety and equal opportunities. In addition, there may be other statements that learners may encounter in the world of work.

Health and safety

For most organisations, the health and safety of employees is of the utmost importance. This is not only concern for the welfare of employees, but also enlightened self-interest as so many working days are lost each year through causes attributable to poor health and unsafe practices. A reputation for safe working is good for employers and employees. Yet many learners enter the world of work without any foreknowledge of this crucial area.

Equal opportunities

Unlike health and safety legislation, which has a largely practical basis and is only partially a moral consideration, equal opportunities law is almost entirely moral with a contentious practical dimension. It is designed to ensure that people are not disqualified from any aspect of work on account of their sex, religion or colour. However admirable this may be, it is notoriously difficult to administer in practice.

In trying to give a realistic edge to equal opportunities legislation, employers publish policies that set out their attitudes explicitly. Employers, when recruiting, making promotions and dealing with employees on a daily basis, are expected to be guided by the policy. Employees should also take note of the principles of the policy during their work activities.

Stop and think: Key organisational policies

Do you know where your organisation's equal opportunities policy is displayed?

What are its main provisions? How aware are you of the principles of equal opportunities guiding the activities of your school? How far are learners made aware of these issues?

Other policies

There are other policies relating to work published by employers and other organisations. In your workplace, for example, there may be a learners' charter, which is part of an overall school mission statement, or guarantees about how rapidly the school should respond to external contacts and requests for information.

WHAT CAN TEACHERS DO?

1 Use work-experience to promote understanding of the vital areas of working life described above.

2 Review the growing literature concerning the differences in performance between boys and girls at school and consider how many of the techniques suggested in this book could contribute to a policy that challenges gender-based imbalances.

SUMMARY

◆ AS THE PACE OF CHANGE INCREASES, THE SKILLS DEMANDED OF YOUNG PEOPLE LEAVING SCHOOL ARE LESS PREDICTABLE.

◆ THE DEVELOPMENT OF TRANSFERABLE SKILLS AND A WILLINGNESS TO EMBRACE LIFELONG LEARNING ARE INCREASINGLY DESIRABLE.

A learning framework

In Section Twelve we learn that:

● *Learning is most effective when it takes place within an explicit framework.*

● *The stages of the Learner's Journey can be reflected at the level of the lesson, the term or the academic year.*

Most human activities that extend over time develop structures that help us to organise and make sense of experience. In schools, we organise our days explicitly around a timetable, academic years fall into terms and learner development is surveyed at key stages. The Learner's Journey suggests that there is a hidden structure to a learning 'career', which unconsciously guides teachers and students along a particular path. This final Section attempts to summarise and draw together the main themes of the book and then considers how to translate them into a practical framework that can guide teachers' actions.

The three elements of the framework are:

● learning principles

● learning contexts

● learning design.

Learning principles

Learning principles and learning contexts are considered in detail in Section Six (page 83). The learning principles are:

● individual accountability

● co-operation

● visibility

● safety.

Our emotions are a major influence on what, how and how much we learn. Learners arrive at the classroom door with a 'history' of experiences, both good and bad, arising from their life within and outside the school. Being 'safe' is a relative feeling, but teachers have a key role to play in making learning a positive experience for everyone and still maintaining high expectations of each individual.

Do not forget the importance of creating the right emotional atmosphere in your classroom. This is essential if learners are to feel safe in taking risks, and making the mistakes that lead to intellectual growth.

The way you look, stand and move all convey messages to learners. Students will read confidence, or lack of it, far more readily from your body language than from what you say. The very best public speakers give individuals in an audience the impression that they are speaking personally to them. The same effect should be possible for the teacher by:

- making repeated eye contact with everyone in the group

- avoiding distracting habits such as twirling rings on fingers, fiddling with paper clips, jingling keys in pockets or pointing with marker pens (your audience will be perpetually waiting for you to mark your clothes or your face!).

By all means move about the room, but stay still for most of the time you are speaking. Remember to use the 'V of attention' (see the diagram below). From the front of the room, your eye will take in only a limited sector of the group, so move around or turn your head around to vary the point of view. Do not neglect learners at the edge of the 'V'.

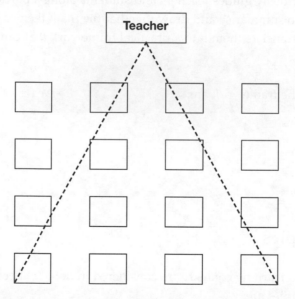

Remember to maintain eye contact if you want to control proceedings and channel all interactions through you. Drop eye contact if you want members of the group to begin interacting with each other.

Learning contexts

The learning contexts discussed in Section Six (page 86) are:

- one-to-many ('whole-class teaching')

- one-to-one (used frequently in some practical lessons, but less often in others)

- one-to-group (where the teacher adopts the role of leader to a small group of learners)

- group work (students collaborate in their learning)

- through resources (the teacher sets tasks that learners fulfil through a variety of print and electronic media).

Stop and think: Principles and contexts

Do you agree that the four principles set out above represent essential guidelines for teaching and learning? Do you agree with the order in which they are presented? For example, do you think 'individual accountability' is the most important?

Are the lists sufficiently comprehensive? Do you think that there should be greater emphasis on one or two of the principles, rather than trying to balance all four?

Are there any other teaching contexts that have been neglected here? To what extent do you use the full range of the contexts in your teaching programmes? How much weighting do you give to each one?

Comment

One of the keys to balancing learning principles and contexts successfully is the use of appropriate learning design. Unfortunately, this is an area frequently neglected by teachers, particularly as they become more experienced. There is a tendency to believe that learning design is for the novice who needs a formal lesson plan. Consequently, as a personal rhythm begins to assert itself, learning design becomes increasingly implicit. One of the key themes of this book is that learning should be visible, and this applies as much to the structure of lessons as to any other aspects of teaching.

The ten stages of the Learner's Journey represent a way of understanding learning as it unfolds over time. They offer a model for describing individual progress and analysing the difficulties learners encounter over the long term.

Learning design

The focus of 'learning design' is on structuring relatively short sessions (40–90 minute lessons), although the labels used could apply equally to modules of work or an entire school career.

As a guide to structuring lessons, teachers may be familiar with the maxim:

> Tell them what you are going to say.
> Tell them.
> Tell them what you have said.

This is useful shorthand that reminds teachers of the benefits of organising material into a beginning, middle and end. However, while it benefits from directness and simplicity, it is far from complete. For example, should the last sentence be amended to '*Agree with them what you have said*'?

A helpful refinement, which reflects the Learner's Journey, might be to organise learning into six stages. Not all lessons can contain all six stages, though most should. One stage may overlap with another and there is considerable room for individual variation and development. However, as a minimum each lesson should have an introduction, a development and a conclusion. We may term this the 'floor'. The 'ceiling' is therefore:

1 inception

2 aims and objectives

3 introduction

4 development

5 reflection

6 conclusion.

Each of the six stages is considered in more detail below.

Inception

Inception may be defined as the atmosphere that you create before and at the very beginning of any lesson. Inception activities are those we use to induce learners to 'cross the threshold'. Whether the teacher designs inception into the learning programme or not, it is always a factor, so it is worth taking the trouble to create the atmosphere that arouses interest in learning. If we want learners to be active, it makes little sense to start the lesson with a passive activity like calling the register.

There are many activities that could be part of the inception of a lesson. These include preparing the room before a session begins, greeting individuals at the door and having work already set out on tables for them to get on with. The importance of good inception activities is their potential for setting the tone of a lesson. Inception activities can turn time that is often lost at the beginning of a lesson because of late arrivals into productive activity for those who are punctual.

Variations in the inception phase can help to build expectations for what is to follow. For example, a board with the single word 'BLOOD' on it might serve as a dramatic introduction to a Biology lesson. It would certainly stimulate thinking while the class is waiting for the lesson to begin.

It has long been recognised that one of the characteristics of learning is that it is more efficient when learners already possess some structures that provide a framework for absorbing new information. The concept of inception could be taken a step further by using 'pre-exposure' for learners, which provides such a framework. For example, a new topic could be introduced by exposing learners to a wall chart that lists key items of vocabulary.

Stop and think: Creative classroom teaching
The 'BLOOD' idea as inception is taken from what is known as 'enigma advertising' where a product is 'trailed' before an audience in such a way that it raises questions in their minds and arouses interest. Can you think of other techniques from external sources that could be borrowed and adapted for classroom use?

WHAT CAN TEACHERS DO?

1   Use 'don't sit down' activities, where you ask learners to undertake a task as they enter the room, perhaps writing a response to a question on the board or on flip chart paper.

2   'Pre-expose' a wall chart with key vocabulary one week before teaching the topic, but make no reference to it at all; give a slip-test on the vocabulary to ascertain how much has been absorbed without any teaching.

3   Meet and greet individuals at the door of your room, encouraging them literally to 'cross the threshold'.

4   Don't say a word as the lesson begins, but have the books and work already set out on the desks and instructions written up on the board.

Clarifying learning aims and objectives

An important element in making learning visible is the setting of clear aims and objectives. These are considered in more detail in Section Three (page 50).

Besides considering aims and objectives, teachers may also want to give some thought to the terms they use in the classroom. A teacher's familiarity with certain terms, apparently of a non-technical nature, can lead to confusion in the mind of the learner. Specific examples of words teachers may wish to review are given below with a suggested definition appropriate to teaching and learning.

explain   give a clear account of a subject, or reasons for a particular course of action

identify   select and name items of a similar group

list   provide a set or group of items without explanation

outline   give the most important features of a subject or idea

Stop and think: Reviewing your language control
Consider the language you use in the classroom. Are the key terms clearly defined for learners?

WHAT CAN TEACHERS DO?

1 Begin lessons by explaining your objectives and conclude with a review of how far they have been achieved.

2 Set aside space for writing objectives and targets (and sometimes aims) on the board.

3 Encourage learners to set personal objectives.

Introduction

The purpose of the introductory stage of learning design is to link new learning to what has gone before, identify the extent of prior knowledge and stimulate interest for the current lesson. Naturally, not all of these will be appropriate for every occasion. However, it is certainly true that fitting new knowledge into a pre-existing framework helps learning.

When introducing a new topic ask learners what they know or have heard about the subject already. Draw attention to the cover illustration of a textbook and invite speculation about what they are going to learn from it. Teachers are often surprised by how much knowledge learners already possess, and learners feel that at least they are not being treated as a blank page.

Every storyteller knows the importance of the first sentence of a narrative. A reader can either be captivated or lost in those opening few words. Consider learners as your 'readers' and pay particular attention to the first sentence that you use to introduce a lesson or topic.

You can introduce the subject of a lesson in a number of ways. One that has already been suggested is to set out your objectives. However, you may occasionally want to use some rhetorical devices. You could:

● recall an anecdote that illustrates your theme

● use a rhetorical question to arouse interest (*'How often have you thought, I wish I was around when ... happened?'*)

● use a shock opening statement (*'Before the Twentieth Century, doctors probably did more harm to their patients than good'*).

WHAT CAN TEACHERS DO?

1 Introduce a new topic by writing a lesson title, an eye-catching word, or number, or drawing a picture on the board before the lesson begins. Ask the group to spend the first few minutes writing down anything that comes into their heads in response.

2 Look for creative openings and endings to lessons in unusual places where 'impact' is important (for example, on television programmes or in advertising).

Development

The development stage represents the focal point for learning and as such will occupy the greatest amount of time in a lesson or module of work. There is a detailed consideration of the techniques appropriate to development in Sections Five to Eight. Within the development stage, the teacher must consider the best way of structuring material. The three basic structures are:

- heuristic
- narrative
- problem solving.

There are a number of possible variations and refinements and, of course, many lessons will combine different elements of these structures.

Heuristic

This approach is one of the oldest in teaching and was the preferred method of Socrates. The teacher proceeds by asking a series of questions that stimulate learners to think for themselves in supplying answers. It is not a good structure for conveying information, but it can excite curiosity even in those who are apparently not participating. Neither should this structure be used for checking whether information has been absorbed since only one person can answer at a time and this may give a distorted picture. Refer to Section Eight for a more detailed consideration of 'testing' and questioning technique.

Narrative

Narrative too is an ancient form of teaching and one of the most commonly performed speech acts of our personal and working lives. We use narrative to describe events in formal and informal settings. It is for this reason that learners need to practise the skill as well as hear it from the expert practitioner.

In classrooms, the teacher explains a sequence of events, a process or succession of cause and effect. Success depends on blending the elements of agents (those who act in the narrative), actions (what happens) and outcomes (the results). There will usually be a need to select the material to be conveyed, omitting some parts. Such editing need not be a distortion; it may just make the narrative more focused or easier to understand.

Problem solving

Problem solving is a technique that helps to promote dialogue between the teacher and the learners. The variation commonly found in business and industry is the 'brain-storming' session. Teachers interested in promoting risk-taking and adventurous thinking may be interested in the basic rules of brain-storming, which are summarised in Table 12.1.

Table 12.1 Rules of brain-storming

Stage	Rule
Stage 1	A problem is stated as clearly as possible.
	Everyone is expected to offer ideas.
	All ideas are written down.
	No ideas are rejected as inappropriate in the early stages.
	Extraordinary, startling, even completely impractical suggestions are encouraged (the idea is to see the subject with fresh insight).
Stage 2 (when the flow of ideas has dried up)	Find 'plus' and 'minus' points for each of the proposed answers/solutions.
	Refine the promising ideas.
	Settle on one (or a combination of several) solution(s).

Stop and think: Which is your preferred approach to teaching?
Teachers instinctively teach in the way that teachers they admired taught them. Is this true of you? Have you considered which style you use and why? Think back over recent lessons. Which technique did you use? Was it really appropriate to the subject matter?

Reflection

Learning benefits from reinforcement. Teachers are well aware of this, but still tend to neglect this aspect of the learning cycle. The most common techniques used for reflection are to set a simple test on the subject matter of the lesson, write up some notes or extend understanding through homework. However, there are other possibilities. For example, the teacher could return to the objectives set at the beginning of the lesson and discuss with the group how far they have been achieved. Another technique is to use a class reaction team or 'response group'. This is a group of students, identified at the beginning of the lesson, whose responsibility it is to ask questions and clarify particular points of understanding (see page 91). Membership of the team should be rotated around the class.

WHAT CAN TEACHERS DO?

1 Reflect on the material in a lesson by discussing mnemonics or using 'memory maps' or other ways to 'make it strange', so that it can be easily remembered.

2 Ask learners to consider how the information is relevant to the world outside the classroom.

Conclusion

The conclusion always comes last! An obvious statement, but many lessons simply end when the bell goes without any clear signal to learners that the session has closed. This may be because:

● teachers and learners lose track of time and are surprised to find that it has run out

● the teacher has misjudged the time needed to deliver the lesson

● on that particular occasion, learning did not fit into a neat package

● of bad management.

Occasional problems like these do not matter as long as the general trend is for lessons to finish on time with an appropriate strategy. Edit your material to fit the time you have available, but if you want to avoid glancing at your watch all the time, have a wall clock fitted where you can see it easily.

WHAT CAN TEACHERS DO?

1 As a conclusion to a lesson, 'trail' the next session by outlining the topic and explaining how it links with the one just finished.

2 Facilitate an orderly dismissal from your room by releasing rows or tables only after they have answered questions relating to the work just done.

3 The four elements of 'aims and objectives', 'introduction', 'development' and 'reflection' could occur in a different order to the one set out above. You could, for example, start with a reflection on what happened in the last lesson before developing the next theme. You do not necessarily need each element in every lesson, but their presence does ensure a balanced approach to learning over the long term.

Stop and think: Which structure for you?

Do you agree that there is a 'floor' (introduction, development and conclusion) and a 'ceiling' (the six stages of inception to conclusion) to learning design?

Think back to your lessons of last week. Whatever your model for learning design, did it apply in all or even the majority of lessons?

Make a chart for yourself, like the one set out in Table 12.2, to analyse how you structured learning in any recent lesson.

Use the same chart to build up ideas of what you can do at each step.

Table 12.2 Chart to analyse current and future practice in learning design

Design element	What I did in my last lesson	Further ideas to fulfil this element in my teaching
inception		
aims and objectives		
introduction		
development		
reflection		
conclusion		

Journey's end

The Learner's Journey comes full circle from the 'ordinary world' to 'closure', as the individual prepares for the next quest. The journey is open at both ends, with learners as birds-of-passage. For the teacher, the origins and the destinations of individual learners are beyond the scope of the school portion of the narrative. *Adventures in Learning* offers the Learner's Journey as one dimension for helping teachers to understand the benefits and pitfalls, the excitements and disappointments, of the school experience.

> ... their orbits come out of space and lay themselves for a short time along ours, and then off they whirl again into the unknown, leaving us with little more than an impression of their reality and a feeling of baffled curiosity as to the mystery of the beginning and end of their being.

William James, on the characters in his brother's novels

SUMMARY

◆ LEARNING DESIGN OFFERS AN EXPLICIT STRUCTURE FOR THE LEARNING EXPERIENCE, WHICH REFLECTS THE LEARNER'S JOURNEY.

◆ ALTHOUGH THERE MAY BE STRUCTURES THAT OPERATE AT A DEEP LEVEL, EACH LEARNER AND INDIVIDUAL TEACHER WILL NAVIGATE HIS OR HER OWN COURSE.

Adventures in Learning *is book 16 of The School Effectiveness Series, which focuses on practical and useful ideas for individual schools and teachers. The series addresses the issues of whole school improvement along with new knowledge about teaching and learning, and offers straightforward solutions that teachers can use to make life more rewarding for themselves and those they teach.*

Book 1: *Accelerated Learning in the Classroom* by Alistair Smith

- The first book in the UK to apply new knowledge about the brain to classroom practice
- Contains practical methods so teachers can apply accelerated learning theories to their own classrooms
- Aims to increase the pace of learning and deepen understanding
- Includes advice on how to create the ideal environment for learning and how to help learners fulfil their potential
- Full of lively illustrations, diagrams and plans
- Offers practical solutions on improving performance, motivation and understanding
- Contains a checklist of action points for the classroom – 21 ways to improve learning

Book 2: *Effective Learning Activities* by Chris Dickinson

- An essential teaching guide which focuses on practical activities to improve learning
- Aims to improve results through effective learning, which will raise achievement, deepen understanding, promote self-esteem and improve motivation
- Includes activities which are designed to promote differentiation and understanding
- Offers advice on how to maximise the use of available – and limited – resources
- Includes activities suitable for GCSE, National Curriculum, Highers, GSVQ and GNVQ
- From the author of the highly acclaimed 'Differentiation: A Practical Handbook of Classroom Strategies'

Book 3: *Effective Heads of Department* by Phil Jones & Nick Sparks

- An ideal support for Heads of Department looking to develop necessary management skills
- Contains a range of practical systems and approaches; each of the eight sections ends with a 'checklist for action'
- Designed to develop practice in line with OFSTED expectations and DfEE thinking by monitoring and improving quality
- Addresses issues such as managing resources, leadership, learning, departmental planning and making assessment valuable
- Includes useful information for Senior Managers in schools who are looking to enhance the effectiveness of their Heads of Department

Book 4: *Lessons are for Learning* by Mike Hughes

- Brings together the theory of learning with the realities of the classroom environment
- Encourages teachers to reflect on their own classroom practice and challenges them to think about why they teach in the way they do
- Develops a clear picture of what constitutes effective classroom practice
- Offers practical suggestions for activities that bridge the gap between recent developments in the theory of learning and the constraints of classroom teaching
- Ideal for stimulating thought and generating discussion
- Written by a practising teacher who has also worked as a teaching advisor, a PGCE co-ordinator and an OFSTED inspector

Book 5: *Effective Learning in Science* by Paul Denley and Keith Bishop

- Looks at planning for effective learning within the context of science
- Encourages discussion about the aims and purposes in teaching science and the role of subject knowledge in effective teaching
- Tackles issues such as planning for effective learning, the use of resources and other relevant management issues
- Offers help in the development of a departmental plan to revise schemes of work, resources and classroom strategies, in order to make learning and teaching more effective
- Ideal for any science department aiming to increase performance and improve results

Book 6: *Raising Boys' Achievement* by Jon Pickering

- Addresses the causes of boys' underachievement and offers possible solutions
- Focuses the search for causes and solutions on teachers working in the classrooms
- Looks at examples of good practice in schools to help guide the planning and implementation of strategies to raise achievement
- Offers practical, 'real' solutions along with tried and tested training suggestions
- Ideal as a basis for INSET or as a guide to practical activities for classroom teachers

Book 7: *Effective Provision for Able & Talented Children* by Barry Teare

- Basic theory, necessary procedures and turning theory into practice
- Main methods of identifying the able and talented
- Concerns about achievement and appropriate strategies to raise achievement
- The role of the classroom teacher, monitoring and evaluation techniques
- Practical enrichment activities and appropriate resources

Book 8: *Effective Careers Education & Guidance* by Andrew Edwards and Anthony Barnes

- Strategic planning of the careers programme as part of the wider curriculum
- Practical consideration of managing careers education and guidance
- Practical activities for reflection and personal learning, and case studies where such activities have been used
- Aspects of guidance and counselling involved in helping students to understand their own capabilities and form career plans
- Strategies for reviewing and developing existing practice

Book 9: *Best behaviour and Best behaviour FIRST AID* by
Peter Relf, Rod Hirst, Jan Richardson and Georgina Youdell
- Provides support for those who seek starting points for effective behaviour management, for individual teachers and for middle and senior managers
- Focuses on practical and useful ideas for individual schools and teachers

Best behaviour FIRST AID
(pack of 5 booklets)
- Provides strategies to cope with aggression, defiance and disturbance
- Straightforward action points for self-esteem

Book 10: *The Effective School Governor* by David Marriott
(including free audio tape)

- Straightforward guidance on how to fulfil a governor's role and responsibilities
- Develops your personal effectiveness as an individual governor
- Practical support on how to be an effective member of the governing team
- Audio tape for use in car or at home

Book 11: *Improving Personal Effectiveness for Managers in Schools* by James Johnson

- An invaluable resource for new and experienced teachers in both primary and secondary schools
- Contains practical strategies for improving leadership and management skills
- Focuses on self-management skills, managing difficult situations, working under pressure, developing confidence, creating a team ethos and communicating effectively

Book 12: *Making Pupil Data Powerful* by Maggie Pringle and Tony Cobb

- Shows teachers in primary, middle and secondary schools how to interpret pupils' performance data and how to use it to enhance teaching and learning
- Provides practical advice on analysing performance and learning behaviours, measuring progress, predicting future attainment, setting targets and ensuring continuity and progression
- Explains how to interpret national initiatives on data-analysis, benchmarking and target-setting, and to ensure that these have value in the classroom

Book 13: *Closing the Learning Gap* by Mike Hughes

- Helps teachers, departments and schools to close the Learning Gap between what we know about effective learning and what actually goes on in the classroom
- Encourages teachers to reflect on the ways in which they teach, and to identify and implement strategies for improving their practice
- Helps teachers to apply recent research findings about the brain and learning
- Full of practical advice and real, tested strategies for improvement
- Written by a teacher, for teachers, to stimulate thought and interest 'at a glance'

Book 14: *Getting Started* by Henry Leibling

- Provides invaluable advice for Newly Qualified Teachers (NQTs) during the three-term induction period that comprises their first year of teaching
- Advice includes strategies on how to get to know the school and the new pupils, how to work with induction tutors, and when to ask for help

Book 15: *Leading the Learning School* by Colin Weatherley

The main theme is that the effective leadership of true 'learning schools' involves applying the principles of learning to all levels of educational management:
- Learning – 13 key principles of learning are derived from a survey of up-to-date knowledge of the brain and learning
- Teaching – how to use the key principles of learning to improve teachers' professional knowledge and skills, make the learning environment more supportive and improve the design of learning activities
- Staff Development – how the same principles that should underpin the design and teaching of learning activities for pupils should underpin the design and provision of development activities for teachers
- Organizational Development – how a learning school should be consciously managed according to these same key principles of learning. The section proposes a radical new 'whole brain' approach to Development Planning

Book 17: *Strategies for Closing the Learning Gap* by Mike Hughes with Andy Vass

- Highlights and simplifies key issues emerging from the latest discoveries about how the human brain learns
- Offers proven, practical strategies and suggestions as to how to apply this new research in the classroom, to improve students' learning and help them achieve their full potential
- Written and arranged in the same easy-to-read style as *Closing the Learning Gap*, to encourage teachers to browse through it during 'spare' moments

Book 18: *Classroom Management* by Philip Waterhouse and Chris Dickinson

- Classic best-selling text by Philip Waterhouse, set in the current context by Chris Dickinson
- Full of practical ideas to help teachers find ways of integrating Key Skills and Thinking Skills into an already overcrowded curriculum
- Shows how Induction Standards, OFSTED requirements and the findings of the Hay McBer report into School Effectiveness can be met or implemented through carefully thought out strategies for the management and organisation of the classroom
- Covers topics including whole-class presentation, dialogue and interactive teaching; teacher-led small group work; classroom layout; interpersonal relationships in the classroom; and collaborative teamwork

ACCELERATED LEARNING SERIES
General Editor: **Alistair Smith**

Accelerated Learning in Practice by Alistair Smith

- The author's second book, which takes Nobel Prize winning brain research into the classroom.
- Structured to help readers access and retain the information necessary to begin to accelerate their own learning and that of the students they teach.
- Contains over 100 learning tools, case studies from 36 schools and an up-to-the-minute resource section
- Includes nine principles of learning based on brain research and the author's seven-stage Accelerated Learning Cycle.

The ALPS Approach: Accelerated Learning in Primary Schools
by Alistair Smith and Nicola Call

- Shows how research on how we learn, collected by Alistair Smith, can be used to great effect in the primary classroom.
- Provides practical and accessible examples of strategies used by highly experienced primary teacher Nicola Call, at a school where the SATs results shot up as a consequence.
- Professional, practical and exhilarating resource that gives readers the opportunity to develop the ALPS approach for themselves and for the children in their care.
- The ALPS approach includes: Exceeding expectation, 'Can-do' learning, Positive performance, Target-setting that works, Using review for recall, Preparing for tests … and much more.

MapWise by Oliver Caviglioli and Ian Harris

- Provides informed access to the most powerful accelerated learning technique around – Model Mapping.
- Shows how mapping can be used to address National Curriculum thinking skills requirements for students of any preferred learning style by infusing thinking into subject teaching.
- Describes how mapping can be used to measure and develop intelligence.
- Explains how mapping supports teacher explanation and student understanding.
- Demonstrates how mapping makes planning, teaching and reviewing easier and more effective.
- Written and illustrated to be lively and engaging, practical and supportive.

The ALPS Resource Book by Alistair Smith and Nicola Call

- Follow-up to the authors' best-selling book *The ALPS Approach*, structured carefully to extend the theoretical and practical advice given in that publication.
- Provides a wealth of photocopiable, 'hands-on' resources for teachers to use in, and outside, the classroom.
- Describes over 1000 useful ideas for teachers to 'accelerate' children's learning, including affirmation posters for your classroom; how to make target-setting easy, fun and useful; rules and guidelines for positive behaviour; writing frames and thinking skills templates; how to help children better understand their brain and get it to work; advice on managing attention and dealing with groups; ten ways to improve test performance; sample school policies; 101 'brain break' activities that connect to learning.

EDUCATION PERSONNEL MANAGEMENT SERIES

These new Education Personnel Management handbooks will help headteachers, senior managers and governors to manage a broad range of personnel issues.

The Well Teacher – management strategies for beating stress, promoting staff health and reducing absence
by Maureen Cooper

- Provides straightforward, practical advice on how to deal strategically with staff absenteeism, which can be so expensive in terms of sick pay and supply cover, through proactively promoting staff health.
- Includes suggestions for reducing stress levels in schools.
- Outlines ways in which to deal with individual cases of staff absence.

Managing Challenging People – dealing with staff conduct
by Bev Curtis and Maureen Cooper

- Deals with managing staff whose conduct gives cause for concern.
- Summarises the employment relationship in schools, as well as those areas of education and employment law relevant to staff discipline.
- Looks at the differences between conduct and capability, and between misconduct and gross misconduct.
- Describes disciplinary and dismissal procedures relating to teaching and non-teaching staff, including headteachers.
- Describes case studies and model procedures, and provides pro-forma letters to help schools with these difficult issues.

Managing Poor Performance – handling staff capability issues
by Bev Curtis and Maureen Cooper

- Explains clearly why capability is important in providing an effective and high quality education for pupils.
- Gives advice on how to identify staff with poor performance, and how to help them improve.
- Outlines the legal position and the role of governors in dealing with the difficult issues surrounding poor performance.
- Details the various stages of formal capability procedures and dismissal hearings.
- Describes case studies and model procedures, and provides pro-forma letters.

FALKIRK COUNCIL
LIBRARY SUPPORT
FOR SCHOOLS

Managing Allegations Against Staff – personnel and child protection issues in schools
by Maureen Cooper

- Provides invaluable advice to headteachers, senior managers and personnel staff on how to deal with the difficult issues arising from accusations made against school employees.
- Shows what schools can do to protect students, while safeguarding employees from the potentially devastating consequences of false allegations.
- Describes real-life case studies.
- Provides a clear outline of the legal background plus a moral code of conduct for staff.

Managing Recruitment and Selection – appointing the best staff
by Bev Curtis and Maureen Cooper

- Guides schools through the legal minefield of anti-discrimination, human rights and other legislation relevant when making appointments.
- Provides senior managers and staffing committees with help in many areas, including developing effective selection procedures, creating job descriptions and personnel specifications, writing better job advertisements and short-listing and interviewing techniques.

Managing Redundancies – dealing with reduction and reorganisation of staff
by Bev Curtis and Maureen Cooper

- Provides guidance in how to handle fairly and carefully the unsettling and sensitive issue of making staff redundant.
- Gives independent advice on keeping staff informed of their options, employment and other relevant legislation, sources of support (including the LEA) and working to the required time-scales.

VISIONS OF EDUCATION SERIES

The Unfinished Revolution by John Abbott and Terry Ryan

- Draws on evidence from the past to show how shifting attitudes in society and politics have shaped Western education systems.
- Argues that what is now needed is a completely fresh approach, designed around evidence about how children actually learn.
- Describes a vision of an education system based on current research into how our brains work, and designed to encourage the autonomous and inventive thinkers and learners that the 21st century demands.
- Essential reading for anyone involved in education and policy making.

THE LITERACY COLLECTION

Helping With Reading by Anne Butterworth and Angela White

- Includes sections on 'Hearing Children Read', Word Recognition' and 'Phonics'.
- Provides precisely focused, easily implemented follow-up activities for pupils who need extra reinforcement of basic reading skills.
- Provides clear, practical and easily implemented activities that directly relate to the National Curriculum and 'Literacy Hour' group work. Ideas and activities can also be incorporated into Individual Education Plans.
- Aims to address current concerns about reading standards and to provide support for classroom assistants and parents helping with the teaching of reading.

Class Talk by Rosemary Sage

- Looks at teacher–student communication and reflects on what is happening in the classroom.
- Looks at how students talk in different classroom situations and evaluates this information in terms of planning children's learning.
- Considers the problems of transmitting meaning to others.
- Discusses and reflects on practical strategies to improve the quality of talking, teaching and learning.

OTHER TITLES FROM NEP

Effective Resources for Able and Talented Children by Barry Teare

- A practical sequel to Barry Teare's Effective Provision for Able and Talented Children (see above), which can nevertheless be used entirely independently.
- Contains a wealth of photocopiable resources for able and talented pupils in both the primary and secondary sectors.
- Provides activities designed to inspire, motivate, challenge and stretch able children, encouraging them to enjoy their true potential.
- Resources are organised into National Curriculum areas, such as Literacy, Science and Humanities, each preceded by a commentary outlining key principles and giving general guidance for teachers.

More Effective Resources for Able and Talented Children by Barry Teare

- A treasury of stimulating and challenging activities to provide excitement and enrichment for more able children of all ages.
- can be used in situations both within and beyond normal classroom lessons, including differentiated homework, summer schools, clubs and competitions.
- All activities are photocopiable and accompanied by comprehensive solutions and notes for teachers.
- Resources are divided into several themes: English and literacy; mathematics and numeracy; science; humanities, citizenship, problem solving, decision making and information processing; modern foreign languages; young children; logical thought; detective work and codes; lateral thinking; competitions.

Imagine That... by Stephen Bowkett

- Hands-on, user-friendly manual for stimulating creative thinking, talking and writing in the classroom.
- Provides over 100 practical and immediately useable classroom activities and games that can be used in isolation, or in combination, to help meet the requirements and standards of the National Curriculum.
- Explores the nature of creative thinking and how this can be effectively driven through an ethos of positive encouragement, mutual support and celebration of success and achievement.
- Empowers children to learn how to learn.

Self-Intelligence by Stephen Bowkett

- Helps explore and develop emotional resourcefulness in teachers and their pupils.
- Aims to help teachers and pupils develop the high-esteem that underpins success in education.

INDEX

A

abilities, mixed groups 89–90
access to learning 8, 89
action plans 80–81, 158
active learning, exam revision 117–18
activists 11–12, *13*, 49
activities 12, 110
advising, teacher's role 62
aims 50, 80, 171
Aladdin 15
allies 83, 100–101
  peer group as 102–4
  resources as 104–12
  teachers as 100, *101*
appraisals of teachers 37, 96, 97, 144
appreciation, of effort 93
archetypes 16–17, 23
asking, teacher's role 62
assessment 8, 110
  performance threshold 40
    standards 147
  self-assessment 37
  see also classroom audit
atmosphere 34
attitudes
  to learning 8, 9–10, 15
  to life 157–9
audio recordings, revision method 119
audits see classroom audits
autonomy in learning 128–30

B

Beauty And The Beast 15
body language, teachers 168
The Body Shop 50
books
  as classroom resources 110
  libraries 111
Boydell, T. *The Learning Company* 31, 101
brain 15
  imaging, memory technique 119
  storming *173*
Branson, Richard 50
Burgoyne, J. *The Learning Company* 31, 101

C

call to action 18, 44
Campbell, Joseph *The Hero With A Thousand Faces* 15
case studies, test techniques 122
Caviglioli, O. *MapWise* 117
CD-ROMs 14

challenges
  of learning 44–5
  realistic 94
channels of learning 8, 13–14, 15
change
  children's response to 44, 76, 77, 78–9
  of lifestyle 156
  in organisations 155–6
  relapses 78–9
  in working life 157–8
charters 33
children
  as mentors 57, 59
  rights and responsibilities 32–3
classroom audit 143–4
  evaluation, learner's perspective 150–52
  implementing changes 150
  methodology 149
  standards and criteria 145–8, 149–50
  summary 149–50
  teacher's role 144–5
classrooms
  atmosphere 168
  children's work 93
  layout 14, 33–4
cloze procedure, test techniques 122–3
coaches, teachers as *101*
cohesion, in learning groups 89
communications technology 32
community
  displays 132
  and school 134
competency review sheet, exam revision 116
conclusion, of lesson 174–5
confirming, teacher's role 63
connections 10
continuing professional development 34–40
continuous learning 155
control of learning 10
co-operation *85*
courses and conferences 38
criteria, classroom audit 144–8, 149–50
criticism, teacher's role 70–71
cultural influences 155

D

deep learners 9–10, 129
definition of learning 9
Dennett, Daniel C. *How To Make Mistakes* 129
development, in lessons 173
diagram labelling, test technique 125
Dickinson, Chris *Classroom Management* 147
differentiation 10, 89
direction, teacher's role 63